'THE DIGITAL ESTATE

Strategies for Competing, Surviving, and Thriving in an Internetworked World

Chuck Martin

McGraw-Hill

New York   San Francisco   Washington, D.C.   Auckland   Bogotá
Caracas   Lisbon   London   Madrid   Mexico City   Milan
Montreal   New Delhi   San Juan   Singapore
Sydney   Tokyo   Toronto

Library of Congress Cataloging-in-Publication Data

Martin, Chuck. (date)
   The digital estate : strategies for competing, surviving, and
thriving in an internetworked world / Charles L. Martin, Jr.
      p.   cm.
  Includes index.
  ISBN 0-07-041045-3 (hardcover)
   1. Business enterprises—Computer networks. 2. Internet (Computer
network) 3. World Wide Web (Information retrieval system)
4. Business enterprises—Communication systems. I. Title.
HD30.37.M368   1996
658´.05467—dc20   96-35271
                                              CIP

McGraw-Hill

*A Division of The **McGraw·Hill** Companies*

1 2   3   4   5   6 7 8 9 0   DOC/DOC   9 0 1 0 9 8 7 6

ISBN 0-07-041045-3

The sponsoring editor for this book was Betsy N. Brown, the editing supervisor was Fred Dahl, and the production supervisor was Suzanne W. B. Rapcavage. It was set in Fairfield by Inkwell Publishing Services.

Printed and bound by R. R. Donnelley and Sons.

 This book is printed on recycled, acid-free paper containing a minimum of 50% recycled, de-inked fiber.

To Teri

CONTENTS

FOREWORD

Recently returning from giving a lecture at a management retreat in the Rocky Mountains, I was caught in a snowstorm. I got into a conversation with our driver, who lives in a village in the region. It turned out he co-owns a small adventure tours business, which organizes group white water rafting, mountain biking, and climbing tours. Most of his business, he says, is international.

I asked him how a three-person company markets to people from countries around the world, and he replied, "About two-thirds of our business comes from the Internet."

Somewhat incredulous and surprised, I listened as he described the Internet to me: how he has a "home page" that enables him to promote his company to people all around the world, how he has thousands of "hot links" that bring bring people to his "Web site," how he can actually construct a custom tour package for them on the "Net," and how they even pay him in advance with a credit card. He communicates with customers using electronic mail and enables them to see "video clips" of where they will be going. He also publishes a newsletter on his Web site. Business is great and growing fast, all because of the Internet.

WELCOME TO THE DIGITAL ESTATE

The traditional media of the Fourth Estate (originally called "the Press") are converging with computing and telecommunications to create nothing less than a new medium of human communications—with the Net at its heart. And, according to Chuck Martin, a New Estate is emerging: those companies and organizations that are creating and exploiting these digital media. I believe his concept is very helpful in bringing clarity to the relentless and often bewildering developments of the new economy.

To date, much attention has been on new media industries themselves—the converging giants and the Internet startups. Fair enough: This new economy sector is huge—a trillion dollars in North America in 1997 alone. But this sector is not synonymous with the Digital Estate. There are traditional technology and media companies that have not yet become part of the new estate. And the new estate extends beyond this sector to embrace companies like that owned by the mountain limo driver.

These companies and organizations are moving beyond the traditional Net applications (often dubbed "brochureware") to what I refer to as the second generation of the Net. In doing so they are creating new businesses or transforming old business models through the digital media. And the gap between the producers of technology and the consumers of technology blurs because every Digital Estate business is both a consumer and a provider.

The first generation of the Web was informational. Companies and other organizations put up their annual reports and marketing materials—brochureware. I find such sites helpful but limited. For example, when I am about to visit with the management of an organization or government leaders of a country, I look up its site to learn more about it. But after the initial exposure, there isn't much reason to return to that site. In most cases I'd prefer an "I Love Lucy" rerun.

Rather than simply providing information, second generation sites are transactional. Some examples:

- Rather than providing customers with information about your vineyard, you enable customers to purchase wine over the Net, as in the case of Virtual Vineyards.

- Rather than advertising your company's jeans on the Net, you enable customers to design and manufacture their own customized jeans using a network—as in the case of the Levi's Personalized Pair Program.

- Rather than simply providing citizens with information about government programs, you create a "virtual agency of entitlements," furnishing those on social assistance with one-stop shopping for their benefits.

- Rather than providing nifty graphics about what a friendly bank you are, you enable customers to create their own personal home page that consolidates all their personal financial information in one place. The Bank of Montreal is a leader in such second generation banking applications.

- Rather than telling customers what a great cola you have, you engage them in a rich, entertaining, interactive environment that creates an ongoing relationship—as in the case of Pepsi.

- Researchers, rather than sending e-mail between colleagues, use a Net-based version of Notes to create rich, ongoing discussion groups of key topics.

- Rather than creating an Intranet with information about the human resource policies of your company, you create a personal home page for each employee where he or or she can, in confidence, review career plans, compensation history, evaluations, and progress.

Because of the transactional basis of second generation applications, they enable a company to change its business model.

For example, rather than marketing your prefab houses to Japanese customers, you enable a customer and architect to design their house on the screen. When the customer makes the purchase, the design goes over the Net to companies who make plumbing, rugs, wallboard, electrical fixtures, etc. In two weeks the house is on a shipping container going over from Vancouver to Tokyo. The whole business model—how products and services are created and marketed—changes.

Encyclopedia Britannica is a second generation application. The company changed its product from a book to a subscription service to a digital directory (as hot links in *Britannica* guide you to other useful sources of information around the world). It changed its distribution channel from physical to digital. (In 1966 the company stopped selling physical encyclopedias door to door.) It changed its customers from individual parents to institutions. (Over two dozen universities signed up, providing unlimited access to the digital *Britannica* for all students.) It changed its organizational structure and culture. (The expert on Mozart also needs to know about Mozart Web sites and hot links, not just the composer himself.) And, of course, it also had to change its business process.

In other words, Britannica had to transform itself for relevance in the digital economy—a far cry from brochureware.

Second generation applications also have different technical requirements. Because they enable digital commerce (the buying and selling of goods and services on the Net), they must be secure and robust, and they must be more available than first generation sites.

They often require better integration of internal databases than first generation sites. The Bank of Montreal, for example, needs to better integrate the islands of applications (found in every bank) to deliver on the promise of a personal home page.

They also exploit the public infrastructure (dubbed the Exonet by the Alliance for Converging Technologies) to execute business. Rather than hooking up computer systems with customers, suppliers, and others, your company can use the growing public utility to conduct business. A century ago, many companies shut down their internal power plants as the public electrical power grid grew, just as companies tomorrow will be able to migrate IT functionality and applications onto the public information infrastructure.

If it is true that this new generation of application maturity and technical capability of the Net is leading to the creation of a new estate, then we should be able to define some new dynamics and new rules for success.

This is Chuck Martin's great contribution. He sheds considerable light on many of the key business issues emerging from the new estate—the impact of the interactive media on the nature of enterprise marketing, advertising, relationship building, branding, creating communities, and the process of business planning—all explained through the actual experience of Digital Estate companies.

The stakes are high for companies to learn from these new estate enterprises that Martin has analyzed. The Digital Estate companies are building the infrastructure for a new economy—changing the way we create wealth and sustain social development. And any organization or society that does not embrace the digital media will quickly fall behind. Punishment for laggards is already proving to be swift. As Martin explains, there is a certain urgency in becoming part of the Digital Estate. As with the Old West, those who get to the digital frontier first get the good homesteads.

On a personal note, it is gratifying for me to see Chuck publish his first book. A couple of years ago, several colleagues of mine decided that there was a need to create a new think tank and research organization for the digital media. We launched the Alliance for Converging Technologies and have been successful in getting the support of several dozen companies who are key players in the new economy. At a rather critical moment I got a call from Chuck, who suggested we meet to see how he might be helpful and how we might collaborate. A fabulous high-bandwidth brainstorming session led to some new directions for the Alliance, and Chuck became an active and effective supporter of our work. We have influenced each other's thinking considerably over this period, and in his recent capacity as an IBM executive Chuck continues to be an active supporter and colleague.

You will feast on the book. Enjoy it. Prosper from it. And, if you haven't done so already, join the Digital Estate.

Don Tapscott

Chair, Alliance for Converging Technologies
dtapscott@mtnlake.com
http://actnet.com

ACKNOWLEDGMENTS

This book could not have been done without the cooperation of the Digital Estate companies, many of whose top executives contributed their precious time and effort to assure the accurate portrayal of their thoughts, for which I am most grateful. This book is intended to spotlight their business actions in hopes that established companies can adapt some of their new thinking and habits.

Three people, to whom I am especially indebted, deserve special thanks: Anna Copeland Wheatley, cofounder of the Silicon Alley-based AlleyCat, who provided invaluable research for the book and with whom I could not have done without; Don Tydeman, for his astute insights in countless brainstorming sessions and for being a constant sounding board for ideas and concepts; and Don Tapscott, *Digital Economy* author and chairman of the Alliance for Converging Technologies, for providing all-around guidance from start to finish.

Others must be included on my thank you list: NetGuide's Jessica Adelson, for awesome introductions throughout Silicon Alley; Diane Gaume, former Circulation Director of *Interactive Age,* for assistance in the direct marketing modeling; Jerry Colonna, Digital Estate venture capitalist; Rick Selvage of IBM for providing room to move; and my friends at the Leigh Speakers' Bureau for helping me spread the word.

I'd also like to thank Steve Larsen, for helping us plod through those tricky business rules of business netiquette, and Janet Stites, the other cofounder of AlleyCat, for help in the Alley knowledge as well as on the netiquette rules.

In addition, for helping get this book to market, in print, and online, I'd like to thank my editor, Betsy Brown and publisher Phil Ruppel for guidance in helping shape the book early on, and to Designer Sharon Reuter, a designer whom I had the great pleasure to work with in the past, for creating the graphics in the book.

In addition, many others helped in various ways, for which I will be forever grateful.

I also offer a special thank you to Leo and Agnes Martin, my parents, for a life of inspiration.

Lastly, but most importantly, I would like to acknowledge the joys of my life, my two little boys, 7-year-old Ryan Martin and 5-year-old Chase Martin, for showing me how fast children can absorb technological evolution, and for keeping my digital and analog lives in perspective.

Chuck Martin

THE BIRTH OF THE DIGITAL ESTATE

A new wind is blowing, and it's from East to West. The result is the marriage of technology to content in the interactive, global environment of the Internet's World Wide Web.

Although 3000 miles apart, most of the business innovation on the Net is coming primarily from two places: the Silicon Valley entrepreneurs, backed by the deep pocketed venture capitalists, and the Silicon Alley content creators of New York's Soho district, where companies are sprouting faster than anyone can count. Although their areas of expertise are worlds apart, these disparate groups—interlinked by the Net—share several common approaches to creating business on the Net.

These people and companies that are developing and exploiting this digital, interactive world comprise the Digital Estate. They are total believers in the coming digital economy, and they will actually make it happen. They *live* where the rubber hits the information highway.

The Digital Estate companies drive and conduct business exclusively in this digital, interactive environment. These companies understand that the Net finally facilitates the marriage of content and technology (Fig. 1-1).

The Digital Estate has the power to transform not only the way people work, play, relate, and relax, it also represents the evolution of a new force in the world market. The immediate nature of the Internet and the electronic transfer of data means that individuals no longer need to wait for information and entertainment to filter through intermediaries.

THE DIGITAL ESTATE   MODEL

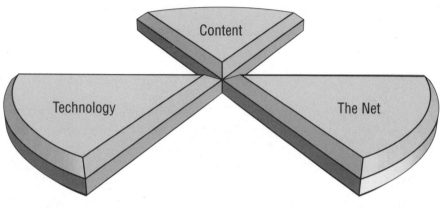

FIGURE 1-1

The idea of an Estate, or an organized group defined by common economic and philosophical interests, derives from the social and political organization of the Estates-General in France. While the French Revolution grew out of a clash among the interests of the first three Estates—the clergy, the nobles, and the peasant/merchant class, the emergence of the Fourth Estate, as the media industry is commonly known, represented a new kind of power based not on class, but on literacy. By uniting the growing numbers of writers, readers, and publishers in France and elsewhere, the Fourth Estate changed the value of information.[1]

Similarly, the Digital Estate is the product of another revolution in how information is produced and how it is distributed, and reflects a shift away from mediated information to instant, individual access.

When it comes to the Net, the business world can be divided into two kinds of people: those who get it and those who don't. More precisely, they are those who believe it and those who don't. From the Valley to the Alley, the leading Digital Estate companies display a passionate belief that the commercialization of the Net and the magnitude of the coming business opportunity are nothing short of a revolution. They view the movement, now that it's started, as having the potential for shifts of astronomical proportions in how we work, live, and play. At the other side, some leaders of established companies view the Net as important but not necessarily critical to their future business success.

As the CEO of a Fortune 500 company said, "Why did this have to happen on my watch?" This gap in thinking and approach only adds to the seemingly chaotic market dynamics. One of the prime lessons from the leaders of the Digital Estate to the leaders of the established companies is this: Don't think that because you don't see it, it's not happening.

Why is there such a dramatic shortfall in thinking? One reason is the newness of the commercial Net. The first Web sites, which were nothing more than static home pages, appeared in 1994. Companies flocked to the Web in 1995, and by 1996 every company had to have an Internet presence. When full interactivity, even without full bandwidth, entered the picture, usage exploded, as consumers and businesses realized that they could communicate with various select groups and individuals whenever and wherever they wanted. New access to new information became increasingly widespread.

Many established companies approached the environment as a new medium in which they could extend their traditional business. With no previous core business, the Digital Estate companies do not have to contend with any kind of corporate legacy; they have no previous brand to extend or leverage. Starting at ground zero, they see and seize opportunity after opportunity. These range from creating new technologies to providing companies and consumers with easier access to information, products, and services. New businesses and categories of business were started: The need for easy-to-use graphical browsers made Netscape famous. The need to find things more easily on the Net made search technology companies such as Yahoo!, InfoSeek, Excite, and Lycos famous. The need for content spurred the launches of countless companies who created new content, communities, and access to products and services.

The established companies, most notably media companies, with decades of experience in creating and distributing valuable content, embraced the Web as a new distribution medium. Such notable brand companies as Time Warner, The New York Times, Paramount, Disney, and CNN entered the market with substantial, content-rich supersites that, in many cases, aggregated the companies' best brands under one umbrella. New content providers, such as iVillage in New York and CNET in California, entered with new types of content, with different viewpoints, and with different methods of organizing audiences.

With fame came fortune. In one of the hottest stock offerings in history, Netscape raised millions for its investors, employees, and shareholders. The money went back into the business: into the Net.

THE LESSONS LEARNED

The leading companies in the Digital Estate approach the interactive environment as a totally new environment, with new rules and operating procedures. The lessons from these leading companies in the Digital Estate fall into three categories:

1. New thinking
2. New actions
3. Keeping the engines running

NEW THINKING

Philosophically, how do the Digital Estate companies approach the Net? What do they really feel, deep down, that this phenomenon is all about? How do they think their businesses should participate? Many leaders of these companies view the Net as the most significant of all paradigm shifts. They are always looking over their shoulders.

- Companies in the Digital Estate easily create and embrace new concepts. Upon startup, I/PRO (Internet Profiles) launched the product into the marketplace because it foresaw that the Net would experience explosive growth and software would be needed to track what users viewed. They launched the product before it was fully baked, kept incorporating market feedback until it was right, kept modifying the product on the fly, and won market acceptance, because the market participated in the creation of the product. When Silicon Alley-based Site Specific started, the company was built in a modular fashion and structured with the assumption that change is the rule. The company organization and work habits are communal in nature.

- Since the Net comprises thousands of vertical niches, Digital Estate companies think small so that they can create large opportunities. They can create markets of everything from Nail Show, for consumers interested in acrylic nails, to the Niche Directory, a series of search engines that focus on particular subjects. They think in terms of small transactions, paid for with digital money. SportsLine uses digital change to cash in on celebrity chats with superstars such as Michael Jordan. Rocket Science Games runs a virtual arcade where Internet users play video games for an electronic quarter, supplied by CyberCash.

- Companies in the Digital Estate think in terms of communities of interactive audiences, and they view the aggregation of these audiences and the discussions they create as programming for the new generation. In chatting, the people provide the content, and the companies sell advertising and sponsorships to companies to appear in those environments. Digital Estate companies think and create products at the grassroots level.

- They think globally since the Net has no geographical limitations. There will be growth in the business of creating platforms for others to join in executing transactions, providing service, or supplying information. As examples, Effect Inc. in Tokyo set up virtual companies through its Web site to support venture business people and a Maryland firm launched Central Europe Online. The Talent Network created a global platform for finding technical, performing, and modeling talent.

- Digital Estate companies understand that, as a medium, the Net is neither broadcast nor narrowcast. Consumers cast about the

Net and pull in the desired information. Companies have found ways to productively use this new, interactive dynamic to their advantage.

- These companies think about customer relationships all the time, and create products and services that empower users. They have created home shopping services, such as Peapod, where consumers pay a monthly fee and a charge per order and like it. They create services like Firefly, which furnishes users with their own intelligent agents that learn their musical likes and dislikes and make personalized musical recommendations. The Web site attracted hundreds of thousands of users.

- Finally, the Digital Estate companies think about vision, or their end game. They have a concrete idea of where they are going. They think of the Internet as the circulatory system of the digital economy. The CEOs of these companies are, for the most part, highly focused and full of drive.

NEW ACTIONS

What actions should companies take to move their thinking forward into online services or products? Companies ramp their businesses in line with the new thinking. Exponential growth, dynamic business models, new collaborative efforts, and new partnerships are the norm. They expect to thrive in an intensely competitive market.

- The Digital Estate companies quickly create new brands in cyberspace with aggressive promotion and advertising. SportsLine created a service devoted exclusively to sports information, entertainment, and merchandise. It offers up-to-the-minute scores, contests, real-time chats with sports figures, and sports shopping. ESPNET and Starwave created SportsZone, a totally comprehensive sports location, with 20,000 electronic pages of information. Lycos, the search engine company, created an in-depth directory of the World Wide Web, and RealAudio created technology that allowed consumers to hear audio over the Net in real time.

- Digital Estate companies target the masses, one at a time and from the inside out. They play to the concept of the Net's being a consumer centric world, with the market of one, at the highest moment of value, as the true target.

- They take customer empowerment to new levels, getting the customers actually to perform the work and even create the products. Lombard Institutional Brokerage uses the Net to allow personal computers to resemble the same terminal look and feel of traders at large investment houses. Companies are also deploying intranets—internal, Web-compatible, company networks that use the Internet to build enterprisewide networks. The benefits are compelling, with inexpensive and global capabilities.

- The Digital Estate companies understand that while any company in the Digital Estate is de facto a content provider, it is context, not content, that is king. In addition to their listings of properties for sale, real estate companies can include city facts and highlights and interactive maps of surrounding areas, with restaurants, schools, and churches.

- These companies collaborate and partner like never before, and live in what is sometimes described as Net Time, the high speed at which things seem to happen in the Net environment. It is a collaboration of enormous proportions involving global cooperation among companies in different as well in as competing industries. In the Digital Estate, it is not a matter of *if*, but *how fast*, virtual commerce will take off, with the expected global, mass usage of digital money.

KEEPING THE ENGINES RUNNING

In the ultimate quest to get it right, the business model is constantly monitored, re-evaluated, and re-jiggered—sometimes daily. Not all companies will make it, and it hasn't been a smooth trip for those that have.

- One of the most difficult challenges in the Digital Estate is how an established company makes the transition to compete in this interactive environment, when its biggest customers and core business don't seem to depend on it.

- Many of the Digital Estate companies have hit bumps along the I-Way. They are becoming masters of what I call mistake learning and of mislearning. These companies have learned how to evaluate mistakes in the context of what it teaches them about working in the new environment.

- The Net's potential for commercial cultivation carries with it a responsibility. Privacy, intellectual property rights, e-mail, Web designs, and interactivity alter the way Digital Estate companies go about their daily routines, and they generally adhere to the Rules of Business Netiquette dealing with consumers and with one another. The Rules of Business Netiquette make up a standard that goes beyond the more general netiquette norms governing the online behavior of individual users.

- These companies remain optimistic about the future, and they foresee a dramatic increase in the use of digital money, an explosion in electronic commerce, a medium for the mainstream.

AN ESTATE WITH ATTITUDE

For the people in the Digital Estate companies, it's a winner-take-all proposition. They feel they will either succeed and be wildly successful or splatter like a bug on the windshield—and they are prepared for either outcome. Job security and viewing what they do as just a job never really enter their minds. The effort is not about making a salary; it's about a pure embodiment of the American dream. The attitude is: "If it succeeds, I become rich; if it fails, I 'die,' and I'm prepared for either."

These companies are created on this basis. As a result, when a Digital Estate company goes up against an established company, the contest is perceived as the revolutionaries versus the mercenaries. For example, if a special project requires employees to work straight through a four-day holiday weekend, pulling 18- hour days, no one considers it an issue. In contrast, in a large, established company, this kind of effort is not the norm. In addition, the amount of money it would cost a large company to make that kind of effort far exceeds what it costs a Digital Estate company. For the bigger company, there is not an equivalent reward/risk factor.

The Digital Estate companies are hungry and passionate. It's not just about money, it's about conviction. When a company gets $10 million of capital financing, the employees still take a bus or subway across town to a business meeting because it's cheaper. In bigger companies, it takes mandates from the top to cut expenses. There's no caviar and champagne taste in the Digital Estate companies, which is one of the appeals to the venture capital firms: It's all about shareholder equity. The only currency is stock. It allows a small company to stare down a larger company and dare it to blink. It's another reason so many young people are in the industry; because they can afford to take the risk.

Digital Estate companies believe that they can grow dramatically and exponentially, and that they can get whatever funding is necessary for growth. They believe they have an edge over established companies, which are either no longer facile or simply can't understand or operate effectively in the Net environment. Deep down, they truly believe they can *win*.

The business community already has reached critical mass on the Net. Ultimately all companies will be part of the Digital Estate, or be dead. What follows identifies the successful strategies of the Digital Estate companies, shares some of their thinking, and helps businesses deal with the challenges and opportunities provided by the Internet's World Wide Web as we move to an internetworked world. Companies can compete, survive, thrive, and (yes) even make money in the Digital Estate—lessons that the current member companies already know well.

LIVING OUTSIDE THE BOX

Ariel Poler first got the idea for I/PRO after publishing a restaurant guide for the San Francisco area on the Net.[1] Advertisers kept asking him what kind of a response it was receiving. Since he didn't know, he set out to track the numbers and ended up with a product and a company. In less than one year, I/PRO was the leading provider of services and software for the independent measurement and analysis of Web site usage. The company secured strategic partnerships with Nielsen Media Research, the television audience information service, and EIT, a Web technology provider working on standards for securing Internet commerce. The success of the company can also be judged by its client list. It includes Microsoft, which used I/PRO to measure the Windows 95 launch on the Internet, and by CompuServe, which used I/PRO to keep track during its $1 Million Internet Scavenger Hunt.

How did he do it? How did Ariel Poler go from a one-man operation to president of a company with 85 employees, contracts with 500 Web sites, and projected earnings over the next five years of hundreds of millions of dollars? Poler's approach is akin to that of the early personal computer industry pioneers. He didn't have an exact business model, but he had an idea for solving what he thought would become a major problem as the market expanded. He decided that the Web really needed the equivalent of a supermarket scanner, a digital tracking system capable of reading and storing all kinds of data. In typical Silicon Valley tradition, he worked long days and nights learning the market, developing a

THE DIGITAL ESTATE

PRODUCT APPROACH

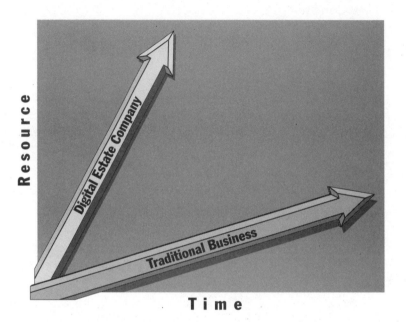

FIGURE 2-1

product, and aligning with the major players. Then, in December 1994, Poler got venture capital funding to start the business.

Poler, a 29-year-old graduate of the Stanford Business School with a touch for technology and 20/20 Net vision, approached business with a total willingness to embrace new concepts, a prevalent attitude of the Digital Estate. For him, working is not just about building new business models. It is also about stepping back, finding new ways of thinking and new philosophies for a totally new medium, which people like Poler view more as a movement. "Somebody pointed me to the Web in late '93 and I was totally blown away," says Poler. "It was a clear and powerful thing."

The leaders of the Digital Estate are acutely aware of the speed of their actions, whether hiring, creating product, marketing, selling, launching product, signing alliances, or filing for an IPO. Time is on their side, but only if they can move faster and more aggressively than the larger or better financed companies. "Large companies build an infrastructure to run things, not build things," says Poler. "They don't realize how big this thing is in the long term. You have to run as fast as you can, listen to the market, then just take what it says and turn it into products. You need the right combination of guidance and feedback."

Trekking around the country, Poler convinced Time Inc., Interactive Age, Playboy, Ziff-Davis, Sun, and Yahoo! to agree to be beta testers of the I/PRO system. Then he began to leverage those brand names to get others to sign up. Many computer publications ran stories about I/PRO and its tracking system. When the daily newspapers and general interest magazines started to take note of the Internet and advertising, I/PRO's name almost always came up. I/PRO kept signing up new members, until Poler and the company's three employees couldn't handle any more requests. From its start in 1995, I/PRO was the instant market leader, ahead of competitors, which announced and launched similar products shortly after I/PRO launched its product.

LAUNCH-AND-LEARN STRATEGY

When he started, Poler began by making a shrewd choice. Rather than design, build, test, and perfect his product before launching it into the marketplace, he opted for what I call the launch-and-learn strategy. "We said let's get started, even though we were small, then let's keep moving forward. We figured that on the Net, the companies best positioned to be successful in the future are those that are successful in the present. We wanted to be successful right away."

Launch-and-learn is so typical of Digital Estate companies and so atypical of established businesses, that it gives the new-thinking companies a constant edge. Companies in Silicon Valley and Silicon Alley often show open disdain for large companies, because of this inability to adapt to the new and constantly changing business models that are a way of life in the digital environment.

Established companies, with processes and policies designed to protect shareholders and owners, are not well-suited for launch-and-learn. Unfortunately, the more traditional approach, learn then launch, runs counter to the speed of the product cycle in the Digital Estate. There is a commonality of certain approaches to business, as shown in Table 2-1. More often than not, members of the Digital Estate simply plunge directly into the business and into the market, to test on-the-fly. The pilot launch of a product is the launch of the product itself. Since the medium itself is in a state of constant change, Digital Estate companies decide to ride with the change and to learn from it. They become companies of dynamic learning. These learning organizations then become part of the fabric of the Web itself, which further fuels their need for speed and for constant growth. For serious players in this arena, this kind of thinking is paramount. Once a company recognizes and accepts this principle, it can move more adeptly in the market. Companies like I/PRO grasped this concept early. The market easily forgives these companies and rarely holds them accountable for abrupt change, since they are viewed as pioneers. When an established company launches a new product, the market expects that the idea, product, and market testing are all fully baked. Those companies are not allowed to waffle on strategy, which could even

TABLE 2-1   Doing Business in Digital Estate and Traditional Companies

ISSUE	TRADITIONAL APPROACH	DIGITAL ESTATE
New product strategy	Learn-and-launch	Launch-and-learn
Research	Prior to launch	Part of launch
Committees	Yes	No
Meetings	Many	Few
Speed of everything	Slow–average	High–extreme
Alliances	When necessary	Fundamental
Business plan	Sometimes rigid	Always fluid
5-year-plan	For accountability	For funding, vision
Employee technical proficiency	Low–average	High–extreme
Executive technical proficiency	Low–low/medium	High–extreme
External contact	Average	High
E-mail usage	Yes	Lifeblood
Perspective of the Net	A potentially big deal	A revolution

affect stock or valuation. They rarely can revise plans quickly or be reactive, because it threatens their market credibility.

When Net-based companies decide to move, they move quickly and decisively. (See Fig. 2-1.) People like Poler believe they have to get their product to market first, even though it might not be perfect. But by getting it out, Poler received plenty of feedback, including criticism from prospective core customers. He took the criticism, modified the product, and kept modifying it as he went, so that the market ultimately accepted it. Poler believes that doing business through the Net entails two methods for success: either remove uncertainty or make a bet. Poler's model was to remove any uncertainty he could. "Companies should take either one side or the other. Those who do a little of each will fail." He also suggests that companies determine how they can do their business better using the Web. "One of the things that made us successful was being very straightforward and honest with the rest of the industry. You need to explain your limitations with your potential customers and partners."

Business concepts ingrained through past business school teachings and experiences collapse in the Net environment. Other than the razor blade industry, who would suggest that giving a product away for free would be a good business plan? More specifically, who would expect that an entire industry could be created in this manner? Established companies need to rigorously evaluate their Net approach to succeed. One of the points of doing business in the environment is that virtually all the rules are different. Traditional business models can't be force-fit. One Silicon Alley CEO likens it to going from a land-based living environment to moving under the ocean. The rules are different, the players are different, and your land-based ideas, no matter how strong and successful on land, simply do not work underwater. The builders of the Digital Estate understand the new, more fluid, environment of cyberspace. They are also realistic enough to understand that it takes more than magic or standard operating procedures to transform aimless surfers into purchasing consumers.

One of the reasons Internet-oriented companies like I/PRO are so aggressive is their view of the interactive future. Poler is no exception: "Five years down the road the number of Web sites will have gone from 50,000 to 500,000, and that's conservative," he says. "I just can't understand how people can see the Web and doubt it. I just can't understand it." Poler warns that if established companies spend too much time focusing on quarterly profit margins, they will miss the boat.

WHAT BUSINESS ARE WE IN?

While Ariel Poler was busy building tools to support the infrastructure of advertising on the Net in San Francisco, another young man was redefining the advertising business back East.[2] Seth Goldstein received his BA from Columbia University in Comparative Literature and got his start in new media producing CD-ROMs. Among his credits is a CD-ROM project with the Frankfurt Ballet and the ZMK Center for Art and Media Technology Karlsruhe, which was exhibited at the Pompidou Center in Paris and at the Interactive Multimedia Festival in Los Angles. At 25, Goldstein found himself working part-time at Agency.Com, a leading interactive ad agency in New York City.

Enter Duracell. The battery company came to town looking for an interactive agency to help create their presence on the Web. Goldstein moonlighted and pitched for the Duracell business. Because of the originality of his thinking, he won the business, beating out large ad agencies such as Ogilvy & Mather. He sold Duracell on the concept that, for a new medium, Duracell needed to build a new kind of relationship with a healthy and creative environment. Then Goldstein banded together a group of designers, programmers, writers, and producers and launched SiteSpecific, setting up shop in his own apartment in an area the company calls SoMa, for "South of Macy's."

The Duracell campaign was a success. Using the online media planning group I-Traffic, SiteSpecific first identified Web sites with demographics that matched Duracell's desired markets. Then it seeded them with batteries that burst through a select number of high-volume sites, such as Yahoo!, GNN, Webcrawler, and Internet Underground Music Archives. Unlike the banner approach, which posts an icon on a home page that, when clicked, leads to pictures and product information, the bursting batteries did not announce themselves as advertising. When the battery image was clicked, the page reversed, revealing a circuit cavity filled with Duracell batteries. Home pages powered by Duracell! The concept of the Net running on batteries! The client loved it.

SiteSpecific not only created interactive advertising for companies who want a Web presence, it used the Web to run its entire business. The company viewed the Web simply as a tool from which they could create additional tools to help them in their work. To track projects, the company created a calendar tracking tool on the Web. From the calendar, they built a project management system, so that they could determine the most profitable accounts. Next came a time-tracking system on the Web, so that they could determine billable accountability. Finally, the company realized that they could sell those products to other ad agencies.

Like many other Digital Estate companies, SiteSpecific is a small company with big plans. Under the umbrella of interactive marketing, the company aims not only to promote brand awareness in traditional environments, such as television and print publications, but also to provide extended services including customer research, product development, product testing, customer loyalty programs, training, product support, and transactions.

Leading Digital Estate companies such as SiteSpecific live the dynamics of the Web. They understand that TCP/IP (Transmission Control Protocol/Internet Protocol) is the standard that will envelope corporations' internal computer systems, because it creates the most open of open computing environments. It is the great enabler that can facilitate the flow of information both to employees and to customers. Another distinguishing feature of the Digital Estate is how well almost all of the workers in these companies fully understand and heavily utilize the technology of the Internet. Hypertext Markup Language (HTML) in the hands of employees is the equivalent of the first copies of Lotus 1-2-3 in the hands of accountants and chief financial officers. SiteSpecific capitalized on its Internet know-how and quick success by aggressively positioning itself to take advantage of the growth of intranets in corporate America.

One measure of SiteSpecific's success came with the announce-ment only six months after formation that direct marketing giant Harte-Hanks Communications, Inc. would acquire a minority stake in the company. Other early coups included serving as a pod for the global book-CD-ROM-Internet project "24 Hours in CyberSpace."

Seth Goldstein attributes his company's edge to a new way of thinking: "We actually assume that change is the rule, not the ex-ception." To keep up with those changes, the company established an object-oriented approach to the business using teams. While a traditional ad agency departmentalizes its talent, SiteSpecific be-lieves in cross-pollinating its talent. Teams are assembled and re-assembled according to the particular requirements for a client. In other words, the talent is clustered around the event, rather than the account. The same team who designed the bursting batteries might not be the same team to design the next Duracell campaign. This approach maximizes the available talent because it distributes talent where it is needed, when it is needed. There is no idle time spent waiting for a particular client to manifest a need for service.

Many companies in the interactive digital environment are communal, partly because employees work long hours in close proximity to each other, as companies economize on space re-quirements during startup. In Silicon Valley, Internet startup com-pany employees sometimes choose to sleep at the office and some-times even have to be forced to take at least one day off a week.

At SiteSpecific, this communal nature lies at the very core of the company's philosophy. Teamwork is neither a trite cliché nor a naive proposition. It is what makes the company work. As Gold-stein explains:

> The Net is flexible and fluid, so we figured we should configure our company the same way. When we had a retreat with all our employees to see where we should go, we found there were no definitive answers, but our objective is clear: to help our clients make money.[3]

He adds, "As for our business model, you can't define it. The Web is changing, so our business model is one of constant change. We're always looking to determine the online value model at stake in each client project."

If you ask Goldstein what business he's in, he'll say it doesn't really matter. It only matters to others. "They want to put us in a box, to say we're this kind, or that kind of company." He says some people look at SiteSpecific as an ad agency, but the firm is anything but that.

> Ad agencies aren't thinking of data, they think of images. Our business model parallels the medium of the Web. It's so natural to us that we're publishers, we're advertisers, we're technologists. It's going with the grain. Business models have to be as fluid as the medium. This is a medium that's bottom up, like a Web. We use the Web to communicate, it's our mode of production, it's our business.

The business of many companies in the Digital Estate mirrors the Web in several ways. They are fast-growth, highly networked, loosely affiliated with other companies, adaptable to the latest technological innovations, and highly fluid. Collaboration among companies often seems to happen as quickly and as easily as Web sites are linked to each other. Companies have a better chance of success in the Net environment when they assume as many of the characteristics of the medium as they can.

Digital Estate companies spend a lot of time in the environment, looking at what others are doing. Because the environment is so intensely competitive and leapfrogging is the norm, all eyes and ears are on the Net at all times. When something new and exciting hits, word is instantly "in the network." The Net is the ultimate in the instantaneous dissemination of new information.

Whether you are running a shoe store in Boise or a major media company in New York, new business thinking is paramount in the Digital Estate. Says Netscape's 24-year-old techno-wizard Marc Andreessen, who wrote the software that drove the Web usage explosion: "I don't know if the previous generation of content providers can absorb all this and get to the other side. Lots won't, and those that do will have to change dramatically. Revenues will drop like a rock."[3]

The same could be said for most businesses who don't embrace new thinking to compete within the Digital Estate.

GETTING TO THE OTHER SIDE

Doing business in the Net environment can be daunting to outsiders. The approach of those on the inside is totally different. Here are some common characteristics for business practices by leaders of the Digital Estate:

- *Living On-the-Fly.* Even if the product isn't totally baked, companies get it into the market as fast as they can. The dynamics of the Net market are so dynamic that a product strategy can't be fully developed without real-time experience, which is best gathered live in this environment.

- *Warp Speed Paranoia.* The pace of operation, internally and externally, is at constant warp speed. These companies always feel as though they are looking over their shoulders to make sure no one is drafting them, or more likely *who* is drafting them. Everyone and everything seem move at the speed of light.

- *Flux Is Good!* These companies understand that the market dynamics are in a constant state of flux and that traditional business approaches don't necessarily work in the Digital Estate. They use change to their advantage.

- *The Ink Never Dries.* The annual budgeting process at large companies is nontransferable to this environment. Business on the Net is not for five-year plans, since it's barely possible to deliver on a one-year plan. Business plans in this environment become guidelines. "In 1995, I redid my budget 10 times and reorganized my staff five times," says Hala Makowska, New Media Director of People Online.[4] And as USA Today's vice president and general manager, Lorraine Cichowski, looking at the end of the first quarter, says: "I'm not sure I could write a business plan for the second half of the year."[5]

- *Tweaking, Tweaking, Tweaking.* Product creation, launch, and market feedback are viewed as integral to the product itself. The successful companies continually tweak their interactive offerings based on constant input from the field, which the companies aggressively solicit.

- *Technology as Friend.* Using state-of-the art technology is standard within the Digital Estate, not only in internal infrastructure, but also in integrating it as part of product offerings.

- *Buddies Everywhere.* Partnering with others is a way of life in this arena. Collaboration often replaces make-or-buy decisions.

To operate in what is a new competitive environment for most companies, new business concepts are required. The fundamental issue of how to look at new business actions around the Net can be likened to photographing a fast-moving vehicle. With a high shutter speed, you can get a snapshot that captures every detail but fails to show movement. This is like the fixed business model. On the other hand, you can take a blurry picture, capturing the speed of movement—the "embrace change" model, as stated earlier. In the Digital Estate, there is no room for the fixed business model, since the medium itself cannot be fixed.

In an established or large company, who is willing to go to the mat with corporate or with the owners to launch a new product on the Net? Who is willing, as Ariel Poler suggests, to "make a bet" without a solid five-year plan? Standard business processes demand solid business plans. The problem is that the Net environment is anything but standard. Yet, the established companies, with their tremendous wealth of resources, stand to gain the most if they can adopt the new thinking of the Digital Estate. But it takes more than thinking outside the box. The Digital Estate leaders live outside the box. All ideas are considered, no matter who in the company has them. Few ideas are considered too trivial or far-fetched for evaluation.

Whether the approach is launch-and-learn, speed of product, or removing uncertainty after product introduction, it all entails embracing change as a fundamental part of doing business.

THINKING SMALL IN THE DIGITAL ESTATE

Just as the Internet is the network of all networks, made up of thousands of smaller networks, its content can be viewed in much the same way. The Net is home to billions of tiny bits of information. It is the amplification of this *smallness* that creates the Internet's *bigness*.

One way to view the World Wide Web is as the world's largest container of millions of vertical niches, with literally thousands of potential pieces of information to address most any topic. But it is much more than a repository of information and data. It is a connective fiber linking millions of people, each of whom, at any given moment, is a consumer. Because it links individuals not only to information but also to other individuals, this digital environment also serves as host to temporary and long-term communities. The Net has no masses, only many millions of individuals, each preselecting what I consider the "universe-of-the-moment." Viewing the Net as a network of very, very small parts—thinking small—can help companies do bigger things.

This viewpoint is particularly advantageous for smaller businesses, which are booming in the United States. Similarly, the potential for more individually-launched services is likely to increase. For instance, one survey found that 65 percent of computers owners would prefer a home office to a dining room set when starting new homes.[1] The survey also found that seven out of ten Americans with computers in their homes view their computers as essential, and 71 percent feel that having a home computer allows them to better balance work and family. As these computers and their owners become linked into the Net, there will be an increase in the need for even more niches of information, providing opportunities for established companies, startups, and small businesses to service the voids.

Unlike the leaders of the Digital Estate, who have developed their business around the emergence of a digital economy, many SOHO (Small Office, Home Office) workers end up in the Digital Estate by default. Their original motive in going online is to take advantage of the functionality and resources of the Net. But many of these workers and business owners discover that the Net actually alters how they perform their jobs and run their businesses. In some cases, it even changes the nature of the business itself by creating new opportunities. For example, one secretary who created and launched a Web site to contract out freelance work was so inundated with requests that she created a full-fledged Internet secretarial service.

The Digital Estate accommodates ambitions of any size, and it can compensate or fluctuate with scale. Small companies and targeted ideas can compete with mega-corporations and global goals, because the Net is well-suited to both. Scale is irrelevant to the resources created by the Net.

OFF THE BOOKMARKED TRACK

Bookmarks are handy Web tools that let users save, or bookmark, sites of interest. Bookmarks can be used both as reminders and as shortcuts. The most popular sites on the Web are also those most likely to be bookmarked. When NetGuideNow!, an e-mail newsletter, asked its subscribers to send in their top ten favorite bookmarks, Netscape, Yahoo!, CNET, and ESPN SportsZone figured prominently in the responses.[2] These sites attract not only big numbers of daily users, they also attract the biggest advertising dollars as well.

High visibility, however, is of low value to many companies either who can't afford the cost of mass exposure or who do not really need it. The Net is loaded with opportunities for aggregating content specifically tailored for a select group of people. Creating communities of common interests is one of the reasons that the

Net exists in the first place. Extending this notion into the commercial arena means that anyone can create, target, and collect revenue just by building a community.

Women's Wire is a San Francisco-based company that designs women's-oriented content. In addition to its own Web site, Women's Wire also maintains content areas for CompuServe and Microsoft Network. Its sites feature some original content, aggregated content, such as news clippings, and a large amount of user-generated content in the form of forum discussion boards and chats. While women do not represent a true niche market because their interests are as diverse as those of the general population, Women's Wire has nevertheless carved out a market based on the diversity of women's interests. The site sponsors areas on business, health, careers, home offices, working mothers, beauty, sports, entertainment, kids, and relationships with advertising from Levis and Revlon.

Another example of virtual, vertical niches is the case of Nail Show. Based on a print publication dedicated to the subject of acrylic nails, Nail Show went online originally as a promotion. The site generated so many calls and letters from online readers that Nail Show added an online subscription form. In less than a month, the publication had sold 2,700 domestic subscriptions at $18 apiece and more than 700 foreign subscriptions at $40 each.

The Web makes it possible for even the most targeted or specialized service or product to reach the widest possible audience at the lowest possible cost. Here are other examples of highly targeted products:

- Hollywood Online was originally designed as a general interest site for consumers wanting to keep up with the latest gossip about the entertainment industry. The idea to localize the service came a couple of years after startup when the company teamed up with the National Association of Theater Owners to provide nationwide movie listings on the Net. The Independent Film Channel teamed with 777-Film to offer regional listings on its Net location. A user in Kenosha, Wisconsin can log on, find out what's playing at a local theater or where a show is playing, buy tickets, and even watch the trailer.

- The Niche Directory is a series of search engines that focus on a particular subject. Unlike the major search engines such as AltaVista and Infoseek, which focus on building the biggest databases, the Niche Directory engines concentrate their searches to bring more targeted results. These range from locating experts in various fields to finding specific products and services, such as building supplies and jewelry.

- Chicago Online is a tribute page to the legendary music group, Chicago. Fans can find online tour information, live question-and-answer sessions with the band, real-time music, video clips, song lyrics, album art, exclusive merchandise offers, and a detailed band history.

- The Website for the Association of Flaming Ford Owners details activities and actions regarding possible safety problems with Ford automobiles in North America because of short circuits in the ignition system. Ford owners find press releases, letters from the company, and recall information.

- Scambusters Web is a site dedicated to fighting Internet scams. Examples of such scams include a charge of $1,000 to register a domain name and a quote of $300,000 to launch a company Web site. Scambusters provides free e-mail for subscribers.

- The Student Market Web is making the price of education a little bit cheaper. The site provides a nationwide list of used textbooks, making it easier for students to find cheap copies of coursebooks and textbooks.

In 1993, Kerry Publishing, publishers of printed restaurant guides, saw the potential of the Net and started signing 10-year exclusive contracts with restaurants across the U.S. for the electronic rights to their menus. In less than three years, the company had locked up more than 1,000 restaurants, on its way to 4,000 within the next eight months. The company decided to transform itself into a Digital Estate company and now expects more than 80 percent of its revenue to come from the online product within five years.

Generally, marketing small targeted products selectively on the Net is more efficient than advertising in high profile, mass market arenas. While the same principle is true for print publications and other industries, the potential reach of the Web dramatically changes the dynamics. The distributive power of the Web and new marketing technologies, such as intelligent search agents, can make it profitable to deliver a product or service to a small audience, especially since so many small communities are on the Net. High-profile marketing is low in value, while low-profile marketing increases the value of the marketing dollar.

NOW YOU SEE IT, NEXT MONTH YOU WON'T

When Bell & Howell scheduled its annual shareholder meeting, it opened its doors to millions. Anyone on the Net could drop in and listen via RealAudio. They could also submit questions to company officials. Listeners tuned in from as far away as London and Tokyo. The session was posted on the company's Web page for about a month so that those who missed the event could access it.

Aggregating temporary communities for scheduled events grows ever more popular on the Net as interactive audio, video, and graphics capabilities increase. Events are a dime a dozen on the Web, although few companies have been as creative as Bell & Howell in using the Net as a public forum. The O.J. Simpson trial, for example, spawned a number of sites dedicated to the minutia of the trial, although later they had little value, and some have even been removed. Others, like Court TV's OJ Central, remain active because the trial still generates interest among the core audience for the company. Similarly, the Superbowl or the Olympics are event-specific and have a limited shelf life. These sites may remain active as archives, but their function as a gathering spot ceases at the close of the event.

The Net's ability to aggregate has been used for less commercial ventures. *The Christian Science Monitor*, for example, created a Web site dedicated to coverage of the war in Bosnia. Commemorative sites have been established for the victims of natural disasters, plane crashes, and random acts of violence.

The same premise that motivates event-specific sites can be turned into a different kind of opportunity in a digital environment.

Narrow focus, another way of thinking small, is a perceptual shift that dismantles the Net into its component parts, what Don Tapscott, author of *The Digital Economy,* has called *molecularization.*[3] Like molecules, which are independent structures that bond with one another in a variety of ways to form different substances, digital data can also be fitted to create different products. This ability to manipulate data gives Digital Estate companies many opportunities to create and mine the vertical markets created by Internet.

By combining the molecular nature of a digital environment with the potential for aggregating targeted audiences, the Net has created a unique business opportunity for what I call the *"momentary business."* In a variation of the launch-and-learn strategy employed so successfully by companies like Netscape, momentary businesses can be characterized as *launch-and-leave* companies. By identifying short-term trends (or creating them) and by treating them as events, these companies can aggregate items from all over the Net and sell them for a season, a week, or a day. Let's take two fictitious scenarios:

SCENARIO ONE: THE GREEN SHOES

Green designer shoes are very hot this season. It is anticipated they will be "in" for about three months, and they're being sold at the major shoe stores. No store is going to carry a grossly disproportionate number of designer green shoes, and each store will not carry all brands. A company creates a momentary business called Green Shoes For Now. The company electronically aggregates all the major green designer shoe manufacturers in the world under one umbrella Web site. Some advertising dollars are spent, network-word-of-mouth takes off, and the site has traffic. At the site a consumer finds every variation of green designer shoes, a one-stop shop. Green Shoes For Now has the shoes delivered to your house, directly from the manufacturer, and charges for the service. Manufacturers that don't participate are not listed. The retailer is disintermediated, but before this is known:

- The consumers have found the largest selection possible and made their purchases.

- The manufacturer has sold more shoes.
- It has been only a negligible drain on retail sales of shoes at any given store.

Then Green Shoes For Now is gone.

SCENARIO TWO: HOLIDAYS FOR NOW

The Holiday Home Page Company generates customer holiday sites for customers all over the world. An Internet reminder service sends out e-mail notes to all customers, past and potential, reminding the reader of an upcoming holiday. Subscribers can even add birth dates, anniversaries, and other personal days of remembrance to their personal file within the Holiday database. On Mother's Day, for example, the user sends out special e-mail invitations inviting Mom, family members, or anyone else to come and visit the site at a designated address. Times can be specified to take advantage of the chat and video conferencing facilities, which are Holiday's premium add-on services. The Mother's Day site is completely personalized. Users have the option of creating their own card pages or choosing from a customizable selection in stock. The site remains active for a specified amount of time and then is removed. Archived records can then be purchased as keepsakes.

In the two scenarios, the "For Now" brand is created, with the content, product, or subject matter the variable. Consumers pay for the service, which is a one-stop shop at the highest moment of value: exactly when the product or information is needed or desired.

Momentary businesses can take full advantage of the Web by aggregating content and traffic in unique ways. Online consumers respond well to anything that saves them time or provides useful service. Momentary businesses can do both. The launch-and-leave strategy is a low-cost alternative to more traditional business models centered around building product or service over time. Flexibility and flickering presence are the ingredients to success for momentary businesses.

KEEP THE CHANGE

Anyone who is tempted to dismiss pennies as annoying pocket change should keep this in mind: A penny doubled every day equals $5,368,709.42 at the end of thirty days as the following chart demonstrates.

Day	Number x 2	Total	Day	Number x 2	Total
One	1	2	Sixteen	32,768	65,536
Two	2	4	Seventeen	65,536	131,072
Three	4	8	Eighteen	131,072	262,144
Four	8	16	Nineteen	262,144	524,288
Five	16	32	Twenty	524,288	1,048,576
Six	32	64	Twenty-one	1,048,576	2,097,152
Seven	64	128	Twenty-two	2,097,152	4,194,304
Eight	128	256	Twenty-three	4,194,304	8,388,608
Nine	256	512	Twenty-four	8,388,608	16,777,216
Ten	512	1024	Twenty-five	16,777,216	33,554,432
Eleven	1024	2048	Twenty-six	33,554,432	67,108,864
Twelve	2048	4096	Twenty-seven	67,108,864	134,217,728
Thirteen	4096	8192	Twenty-eight	134,217,728	368,435,456
Fourteen	8192	16,384	Twenty-nine	368,435,456	536,870,942
Fifteen	16384	32,768	Thirty		$5,368,709.42

Such exponential growth is an essential factor in the Digital Estate where the number of Web pages doubles every 53 days.[4] Not only are more users online, but also new technologies make incremental payments possible. Companies can charge pennies for services that can be utilized by millions. While larger companies, like CompuServe or *The Wall Street Journal*, lean toward tiered subscription fees, as in cable television and premium channels, new options allow any company to cash in on the impulse, small item purchase. Known variously as *microtransactions* or *micropayments*, these digital change machines are the bubble gum dispensers of the Digital Estate.

Microtransactions are a natural extension of digital money. Rather than adopting the credit card model, which requires elaborate billing systems, companies such as CyberCash are creating small payment schemes that gives users the ability to transfer money from a bank account or other money source into a digital purse. Consumers can then carry their digital wallets and make small payments at various sites. As security and privacy issues surrounding the implementation of digital money are ironed out, some companies in the Digital Estate are testing the waters early, hoping to make big profits out of small change.

- SportsLine uses digital change to cash in on the popularity of online celebrity chats. A subscriber pays admission to engage in chat session with superstars like Michael Jordan or Shaquille O'Neal.
- Discovery Online, in exploring the benefits of charging for selective online content, is working with a cable modem service. Discovery charges for video downloads. A subscriber reading an article about French cooking pays 50 cents for a 5-minute video on soufflé making.
- Playboy has opted for the pay-per-view model. Prices vary according to content.
- Rocket Science Games, working with CyberCash, runs a virtual arcade where Internet surfers can play video games for an electronic quarter.
- NLighN, a research database, charges small fees per article accessed. Subscribers search for and receive annotated descriptions of relevant articles. The full text for most articles can be accessed for about a dime.
- A group of young people has devised a Web-based game, along the lines of "Dungeons and Dragons," that uses currency in very small increments. Although the game is distributed free, users must pay a nickel or a dime apiece for things like "bullets" and special clothing for furthering their success in winning the game.
- Small World Games doesn't charge for its services, but the model it uses for its rotisserie-type games is ideally suited for the move to micropayments. The online games, which include baseball, basketball, football, and golf, use a financial model in which users trade stocks for players in an effort to create the ultimate dream team.

- InfoAccess sells Business Profiles of more than 10 million businesses for $3 each. The service provides in-depth information, including credit ratings, on virtually every business, large and small, in the United States. Each profile includes an executive summary of:

The company's operation.

The number of employees.

The company name, address, telephone and fax number.

The estimated sales volume.

Key contacts.

Primary and subsequent lines of business.

Area companies in the same line of business.

Micropayments are an obvious source of revenue, but one that has an extended influence. While the business press is filled with news of giant mergers and acquisitions in almost every industry, the Net is spawning small business opportunities for a growing number of Digital Estate companies that recognize the potential of staying small—at least in focus, if not profits.

THINK SMALL, ACT BIG

Thinking small has a number of advantages in the Digital Estate. At the company level, the distributive power of the Net makes it possible for a company to start out small—a one-person home office—and grow phenomenally. On the product or service level, the Net also makes it possible and, more importantly, profitable to target products and services to smaller numbers. In the Digital Estate, a thousand points of light becomes a billion points of presence. Thinking small also creates business opportunities unique to the Net environment by making possible the temporary and long-term aggregation of products and services.

COMMUNITY RULES

One of the first real obstacles facing a company interested in doing business on the Internet is overcoming the jargon. The task is made more difficult by the proliferation of new technologies and new ways to describe them. In addition to terms such as meg, ram, ports, and motherboards, that were once the clubhouse code of computer professionals, the Internet introduces an equally bewildering array of terms for the uninitiated. Hits, links, bps's, jpegs, gifs, agents, html, java, vrml, and the like are all technical terms to describe the components of the Net.

The jargon aside, it is far more important to recognize that for all its techno-wizardry the Internet is about people, not components. Where there are people, there is always the need for community.

While some say that cyber community isn't real, it in fact has been a fundamental element in the development of the Internet from the beginning. What grew out of the need to connect first military communities, then academic and scientific communities, it is a system whose sole function is to connect people. It is important to recognize that the Internet doesn't do anything more than that. The tricky part comes in trying to figure out what you can do in the spaces and places created by the Net. Whatever the product or service, it is important to keep in mind that in this environment community rules.

THE INTERACTIVE AUDIENCE

The concept of building communities is not exactly a new idea. Local newspapers, trade publications, interest-based magazines, and local

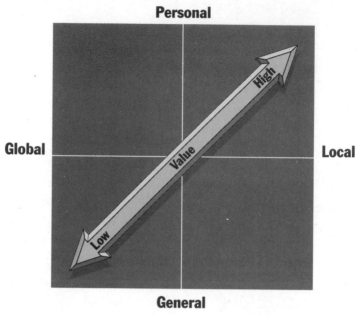

FIGURE 4-1

television and cable markets have been in this business for a long time. So what's new about how the Net builds communities? Everything!

Traditional content providers view their content as a high-value drawing card. In the print publishing world, media companies generally view the aggregation of audiences in one of two ways:

- Geographically, such as local newspapers, which deliver the paper to people in a city or town.
- By special interest, as in the case of magazines geared toward topics such as skiing, tennis, news, and fashion.

In either environment, the publisher creates the information by hiring sometimes large and expensive staffs of writers and editors to create content, and large production staffs to traffic articles and graphic illustrations into print, which can then be packaged, promoted, and distributed. The same holds true for television, where networks and local affiliates concentrate on broad and local geographic distribution, while cable companies such as ESPN or the Lifetime Channel have the flexibility to target interest- and lifestyle-based audiences.

In both cases, consumers have limited options with regard to the content provided. They can buy or not buy the product or service. Thus, consumers have only an indirect influence over the content provided. One letter to the editor or call to a station manager is, for all practical purposes, meaningless. Only in numbers do consumers have any control over content.

The Net, however, is a different kind of medium because it not only allows consumers to sift and surf through staggering loads of content, but it actually empowers them to generate content of their own. More importantly, the concept of user-created content and context is totally consistent with the concept of the Web. The medium exists to connect people. Why not provide people with a reason to connect?

As in traditional media, communities in the Digital Estate are also aggregated by geography, lifestyle, or interest. However, community on the Net is not limited to an either/or proposition. People don't have to limit themselves by interest or geography, nor do they have to limit their choices based on availability and distribution. This audience is neither captive to the content as with print, nor passive recipients of content as with TV. These consumers can and do change their minds, mixing and re-mixing a variety of content that is available to them via the Net. The interactive nature of this environment transforms consumers into active (interactive) participants in the creation of information that they have come to access. In the Digital Estate, it is important to recognize the extent to which the audience ultimately defines and drives content. (See Fig. 4-1.)

BUILDING COMMUNITIES

Klause Rehnig, president of *Medical Tribune*, the leading German newspaper for doctors, built the success of the publication on an unorthodox assumption in the publishing world.[1] His mantra: "That which you can hold up to an audience, and is a mirror of that audience, is the best form of publishing." Rehnig drove *Medical Tribune* to the number one physicians' newspaper in Germany by getting the audience of physicians to write many of the articles in the paper. They weren't news stories, but rather individual commentaries around which the country's community of doctors could rally, either for or against whatever issue was raised. The articles were guaranteed to be the right stories for the audience, since they were written by the audience itself. The paper always covered exactly correct issues at exactly the right time because the issues were raised by the readers at the times they mattered most. The newspaper simply provided the platform, or the conduit, for the dialog.

In doing so, *Medical Tribune* created a passionately loyal following, not because the doctors necessarily thought the paper itself was so great, but because it was the doctors' own community. The paper received the highest readership scores and therefore tens of millions of advertising dollars from pharmaceutical companies that would pay dearly to have the same doctors see their message. In spite of its tremendous success, however, the model used to build the *Medical Tribune* is still the exception, not the rule, in the media world.

In the Digital Estate, however, Rehnig's exception becomes the rule. Digital communities are created in many places. New Jersey has New Jersey Online, New York has Total New York, and people who want to meet other people like themselves have Match.Com. The leading commercial online service, America Online, wants to create its own version of Digital Cities, complete with local movie listings and restaurant reviews, in 200 communities by 1999. That's digital thinking, and precisely the kind of thinking that is making one Silicon Alley startup a success.

GRASS ROOTS DISCUSSIONS

On the fourth floor overlooking Fifth Avenue in New York's Chelsea area, a Silicon Alley startup is working hard to become the premier architect of a new kind of community. The company name says it all: iVillage.[2]

CEO and cofounder Candice Carpenter says the idea for iVillage took shape in response to the original structure of America Online. Carpenter, who is a former president at both Q2 for Time-Life Video and Television, along with her long-time friend Nancy Evans, former editor of *Family Life,* had been invited by the then new online service to help them sort out a new business model. "What we found was that everything was separate," says Carpenter. "You had publications over here, chats over there, merchandise over here, ads over there, bulletin boards here." The women realized that they could create a broad-based area, based on interest, that could utilize all of the aspects of community. AOL, whose on-line strategy has always been to foster a sense of community among its users, agreed to back the project. "We looked at what people care most about and zeroed in on parenting, jobs, health/fitness, relationships, and religion." Deciding that parenting was the most important issue for people with children, iVillage designed and established ParentSoup.

The idea behind ParentSoup was straightforward: Provide an area in which parents could come at any time of day or night to get information and advice on raising their children. The site was organized to facilitate conversations among participants. Local mayors were recruited to help maintain areas by making sure that questions were answered and that individual participants felt at home. Tina Sharkey-Nederlander, Senior Vice President of Programming and Executive Producer, articulates one of the prime directives governing the company's efforts: "You have to be a spark to create a great experience. Engagements are about significant things." And getting people to engage is what iVillage is all about. Among her duties, Sharkey-Nederlander and her team troll the Web looking for potential mayors. They identify people who are interested enough in a subject to address it on a personal home page or discuss it in the various forums and discussion groups scattered throughout the Internet. Her job definition? "I produce conversations."

"The medium is really conversational, so what we're really building is a person-by-person, grass-roots superchannel," says Carpenter. IVillage represents the new model of community creation on the Net, one that echoes Klause Rehnig: "That which you can hold up to an audience, and is a mirror of that audience, is the best form of publishing." By building an environment that encourages and supports conversation, ParentSoup has been able to generate its content from the users themselves. Carpenter correlates this grass-roots approach to an unlikely source. "Alcoholics Anonymous is the best model," she says.

> It's a leaderless community, but not unstructured. It's seamless.
> The quality of interaction is very high. It has strong design, but
> not a single voice dominates. It feels more like architecture than
> content. We're really asking people to come and live here!

While implementing their first goal (to build an interest-based community that nurtures real engagement), iVillage began to see a new way to think about communities. If they could create a virtual environment based on interest, why not cross-section the concept to include geographic communities? "When you try to be national, you bump up against the grain of the Web," says Carpenter. "People have different things to say at the national and the local level. We found a real limitation in just pursuing a national community." IVillage expanded its services to include local areas so that, for instance, a parent in Topeka, Kansas, could talk to other parents in the area about local concerns, such as schools, camps, or doctors.

In addition to maintaining sites on AOL, iVillage decided to brand itself on the Net. The competition promises to be fierce, particularly from the resource-rich storehouses of the larger branded companies. The iVillage team remains, however, undaunted. Sharkey-Nederlander points out that much of what this young company has been doing during its first year in operation is unlearning all the standards that other industries live by. "Every day in this business is like gold," she says. "We have that much more of a head start on whoever is behind us." And while it could easily be argued that a company such as Disney might somehow be able to buy its learning curve by hiring the right people, Carpenter maintains that iVillage will prevail because of its philosophy.

"The Web is a pure democracy," says Sharkey-Nederlander. "Our environment is authored by the people who use it. Our job is not to create content, it's to facilitate communities." In an effort to expand the company dedication to this ideal, iVillage is developing a new set of social technologies called STING. An acronym for Social Technology for Intuitive Navigation and Guidance, STING is the next generation in building communities on the Web. "If you want information," says Sharkey-Nederlander, "you can use a search engine like Yahoo!. But it is much more difficult to find communities on the Web. We wanted to design tools that could be used by the community to build the community." Using database, profile, and agent technologies, STING allows individual users to identify a wide range of topics of interest. Users are then alerted to relevant conversations taking place in both real-time chats and on the message boards.

That the business of iVillage is all about community is reflected even in the organization of the office, which is set up in "communities." Clusters of people huddle around high-resolution, oversized computer monitors, each cluster representing one of the communities iVillage delivers over the Net. Growing from five to eighty employees within a year, iVillage received offers of up to $20 million in financing within six months of launch. It took $11 million from the likes of TCI, the largest cable company in the world, Kleiner-Perkins, the premier technology venture capital firm in Silicon Valley, the Tribune Company, owners of the *Chicago Tribune,* and America Online, the leading commercial online service. Prior to launch, iVillage received advertising sponsorships ranging from $120,000 to $150,000 each per year, from MGM, Nissan, Starbucks, Polaroid, and Toyota. The company projects year-five revenue of $175 million.

The iVillage story is compelling for several reasons, not the least of which is the company's success. Even though the founders began with the idea of building communities on the Net, they also recognized the indelible influence of their years of experience working in print and TV. The willingness to *unlearn* old habits by constantly reevaluating their product lead them to the discoveries that:

1. They could actually center their product around user-generated content.
2. The Net environment is ideally suited for side-stepping the need to make a choice between a horizontal or a vertical market.

In the case of ParentSoup, for example, iVillage can aggregate a community horizontally by facilitating a national discussion of parents of 12-year-old girls. It then can subset that discussion vertically by adding focus specific to one city or town, allowing parents to participate in either or both, as they are most relevant. IVillage can target both markets simply by taking the idea of community as it exists on the Internet to its logical conclusion.

SF SEEKING SM

There are many approaches to creating community on the Net. While iVillage uses the special interest attack with an emphasis on community-type service, others use approaches that leverage specific interests in a single category, such as personal ads. San Francisco-based Electric Classifieds—just south of Market Street in the area once known as Multimedia Gulch, now referred to as Silicon Alley-West—created one such community. Jordan Graham, the energetic and fast-moving president and CEO, tells the story.[3]

> We formed the company in 1993 and received seed funding from a venture capital firm in 1994. The company's original concept was to use the Internet as a new and much better way to deliver interactive multimedia-based classified advertising service by providing sophisticated searching and matching technology, multimedia support, and leverage indirect distribution channels to bring buyers and sellers together. Through our learning about the classifieds marketplace, we discovered how important and lucrative personal ads were to newspapers, especially weekly newspapers and magazines. We believed that with our technology and our understanding of the online classifieds marketplace we could quickly establish a dominant position in online personals and then extend our business into the broader and more traditional classifieds areas, such as autos, careers, computers, real estate, and travel. As a result, we launched our first online classifieds offering, Match.Com, an interactive, multimedia, Web-based personals service. We focused early product development and marketing efforts on identifying and resolving key challenges. For example, especially in early 1995, women were the scarce resource on the Internet, conspicuously absent from any online service. We understood that to

launch a successful matchmaking service we would have to attract women first, then the men would follow. This required strong security and anonymity to make women feel safe. As a result of designing a secured environment, Match.Com enjoys higher overall participation of women (nearly 30 percent) than the Internet and online services as a whole. Another challenge was to ensure a large critical mass of users before beginning to charge subscriptions. We knew that for personals (and any classified application), a large base of member profiles (or ads) is critical to building value. So we introduced the service for free, constantly upgraded the features, and found other Web communities to partner with to gain distribution. With good press, member referrals, the evolving art of online marketing, and our partnerships, we grew to more than 80,000 registered members within a year of our launch. When we started to charge subscriptions to new members, we had built sufficient value—as measured by our installed base of members and our features—that we became one of the only Web-based services successfully charging for content. Within two years of launching, we expect to generate revenues in excess of $15 million per year. Match.Com has rapidly become one of the Internet's fastest growing services and most active Web sites by redefining traditional newspaper personals for the online environment. Newspaper personals require individuals to call the paper, dictate a few lines, with confusing abbreviations, wait for the paper to appear, and then wait again for others to call their assigned 900# voicemail box. On Match.Com, our members place a rich personal profile, often with a picture and detailed information on themselves with who they are looking for, at any time that they find convenient. They are also invited to explore other member profiles immediately, based on their own defined criteria on a number of attributes. They can send anonymous e-mail as soon as they find someone intriguing. And if they need advice, they can consult our e-zine, where they can gain advice on how to make the most of their relationships. Our members are having much more than "virtual relationships," but real interactions leading to real live dates and relationships and marriages. Match.Com has changed the model of traditional passive print personal advertisements into an interactive, self-publishing oriented community where our members daily create dynamically changing content that is both entertaining and a key enabler in delivering a relationship service, which bridges the virtual and physical worlds.

Electric Classifieds represents how a company can use the technological capabilities of the Net. The company's technology platform includes searching, matching, browsing, information warehousing, tracking, customer management, and branding. By viewing the Net as a series of vertical classified markets, Electric Classifieds acts as a facilitator for sellers and buyers, ultimately collecting a toll on the transaction. For example, Electric Classifieds can take a percentage of a fee when a buyer and a seller exchange an e-mail or execute a transaction. It could charge a fee based on time or on transaction, on information transmitted between members, or even on Internet access, if it chose to provide an access service for the members of any of its communities. The company plans to expand its offerings to other areas where buyers and sellers are seeking to find each other.

The company also subscribes to the *launch-and-learn* approach discussed earlier. When Electric Classifieds started Match.Com, it found that it needed five people to support only 20,000 users. These five people answered questions, handled complaints, and provided overall customer support. Once Graham realized that the business would not be efficiently scaleable with this proportion of customer support infrastructure, he asked researchers at Xerox Parc to quickly analyze the interface, conduct usability testing, and accumulate comments and member feedback. Electric Classifieds conducted on-the-fly focus groups, redesigned the system, and, by the time it reached 70,000 users, it required a support staff of only two people.

DEFINING COMMUNITIES ON THE NET

By the year 2000, there are expected to be hundreds of millions of people on the Net.[4] As more and more people go online, digital communities will have even more relevance. It is fast becoming a case of "so many people, so many interests, so little time." While virtual communities won't soon supplant the need for neighbors, parades, ski clubs, and bridge partners, they will supplement these kinds of social gatherings. In the physical world, you can't easily look at a database of people and find a match of your unique interests and theirs. You tend to find people with similar interests within your geographic sphere. However, on the Net, you can not only locate different people in each of your interest areas, but you can communicate directly with them on your own terms and at your leisure.

The variety of communities that can be created on the Net is limited only by imagination and desire. High-rise apartment dwellers can create their own building community. Businesses can create communities of customers, a buyer-seller community. Workers within a company can create gripe communities. Better yet, you can create the employee digital community, in which you participate when appropriate. Some examples:

GEOGRAPHIC COMMUNITY

- In the New Jersey Online community, "residents" can read local restaurant reviews from patrons who have eaten there, type their own reviews online, and participate in discussion groups ranging from sports to local politics. People raise their own issues, such as the widening of a local street that upset one nearby resident, and find all the information about local yard sales for the weekend. Since AT&T is one of the largest employers in the state, New Jersey Online even created a location called The Unofficial AT&T Insider, where people discuss the downsizing of American business, layoffs, unions, job opportunities, and news from or affecting AT&T. New Jersey Online, owned by Newhouse Newspapers, has created the organizational structure for the service, the platform on which New Jersey residents can organize.

- Large, established companies aggressively pursue the local content market with a range of products, some in partnership with local newspapers. Microsoft has CityScape, AT&T financed City Search, AOL initiated Digital Cities, and IBM introduced KOZ.

STATE-OF-MIND COMMUNITY

- Total New York views itself as more of a site for people with a New York state-of-mind. "Just like Seinfeld is about New York," says cofounder Janice Gjertsen.[5] The site features hip design and entertainment-oriented content, while providing basic information for tourists. One surprise to the company was that almost 50 percent of people visiting the Total New York site are from outside the United States. The Net has no boundaries.

SPECIFIC INTEREST COMMUNITY

- *The Camping Community.* Want to lose weight? Need a tennis tune-up? How about something for the entire family? There are camp communities on the Web for all of these. CampingNet, for instance, is a great source for camping information with a searchable database and links to a number of directories.

- *The AMC Community.* For the uninitiated, AMC stands for All My Children, the popular ABC daytime soap. About 3,000 people congregate around the site on a daily basis, to follow in detail the loves and lives of Pine Valley residents. The 21-year-old organizer Dan Kroll established a tight community by providing daily show recaps, character and actor profiles, message boards, sneak previews, and the necessary chat and bulletin board features. The grass-roots effort is now sponsored by advertising and has ABC's permission to reproduce audio and video clips.

- *The Shoe Community.* Rockport shoe owners trade stories about where they wear their Rockports, and participate in virtual activities from golf to a run for the White House.

- *The Appliance Community.* The publisher of the 50-year-old trade publication *Appliance* set up a Web presence to become the electronic gathering place for anything appliance-related.

- *The Security Community.* Started in early 1996, this location is for the electronic security alarm dealer industry.

Competition for the role of community organizer will be substantial. For example, in the town of Greenwich, Connecticut, there are several sites that position themselves as "the" Greenwich source of local information. These range from Virtual Greenwich, a commercial site created by a 22-year-old, with emphasis on shopping at local stores and useful information such as train schedules to New York, to one hosted by the local Chamber of Commerce.

Digital communities are the future lifeblood of the Net. If a community can be conceived, it can be created in this environment. To do so, however, companies must *unlearn* the models that were developed for success in other media. Back in 1994, *Interactive Age* commissioned the Gallup Organization to conduct a nationwide survey of households to see what would cause consumers to "go interactive."[6] The number one reason: to communicate. Access to live, online communications including town meetings, community bulletin boards, and expert advice ranked first as the most important interactive home service to consumers. This sense of belonging is a main driver of the growth of Net usage.

People want the ability to communicate with others who share their interests and concerns. A working parent might want advice on measles or 401(k)s. A jogger might want information on upcoming marathons or the fine points of jogging shoes. Whatever the subject, the Net is uniquely suited to bringing interests together. It's not the glitz, with the technological bells and whistles, that brings people into digital space, but rather the need to connect one person to another. If you think "community," you can more easily figure how your company fits into one—or better yet, can create one.

AGGREGATING THE WORLD

We've been talking about global for a couple of decades, but doing business in the Digital Estate is a virtual, and therefore, a global, undertaking. Since the World Wide Web knows no boundaries and, as its name implies, *is* inherently global, it makes the companies that enter the environment global from the start, as long as they think that way.

Conducting business on an international scale has generally required high resource levels and deep pockets. On the Net, however, a company can sell its products and services to anyone, anywhere, at any time, without leaving the office. A tool plant in Wisconsin can sell hammers and nails to buyers in Beijing without opening a branch office to handle the transaction. A tulip farmer in the Netherlands can set up an international distribution network. Information-filled corporate databases can be unleashed to companies' sales forces and customers in other countries.

No matter how large or small the company, the global barriers that have traditionally limited multinational transactions no longer apply, which may not come naturally for a small company used to doing business only within its geographical community.

THINKING BEYOND BORDERS

When sailors, in the early days of the Renaissance in Europe, set out to establish trade routes, they did so at substantial risk. Three hundred years later, the risk of exploration and international trade

GLOSSARY

Harvesting—Use of intelligent agents to fly through the Web gathering information, pages, or sites of interest. Often done at night.

Repurposing—Taking what is in a print product, such as a magazine or newspaper, and trying to modify and re-use already-paid-for content. Should soon be an abandoned practice.

Shovelware—Taking exactly what is already in print and "shoveling" it on the Web, without much change.

Houndogs—The slick set of navigation software that finds what you are looking for. AKA intelligent search agents.

Extranet—Not to be confused with Internet (The Net for everyone) and Intranets (inside-the-company-only Internets), these are essentially closed networks of interest, riding along the Internet.

Hits—A grossly overused and not so accurate measurement of traffic to a Web site. Each little piece of graphic element on a "page" counts for hits, so one page can contain several hits.

Page View—When a person looks at one page on a Web site.

Splash—That first "killer" page a surfer sees when visiting a site.

Producers—The people who actually do the work of creating the content within a site.

Chat—Communicating over the Net, generally in real time, but not really talking (yet).

Billboard Advertising—Commercial messages contained in boxes, generally at the top or bottom of a screen. Ultimately will be sent to people who actually may find them of interest.

Pages on the Fly—Creating Web pages as they are needed to fit the exact needs of each user.

Clickitis—The propensity to just keep clicking on that mouse. Makes it tough for a company to keep a consumer at its site.

Herding—Corralling users to stay within a site, generally by running ads all over the Web directing users to one location.

Net Time—The speed at which Digital Estate companies operate. Roughly 10-to-1 ratio to an established company's time.

Hyperchange—The extraordinary speed with which business models can change in the Digital Estate.

Mouse Potato—The Net version of the couch potato, but with interactivity. Likely candidates for clickitis.

Cookies—This technology from the browser "tags" the user so that the site "remembers" when the user comes back and what he or she likes to view. Like a fortune cookie.

Dough—The long sought-after holy grail of the Net.

Cooked—What companies who don't get it will be.

led to the formation of the first insurance and investment companies, to financially protect the companies that ventured into distant and often hostile territories. Today, burgeoning global markets, such as Russia and China, highlight the opportunity and challenges of engaging in international trade. Planes may be cheaper and faster than trade ships, but it is still expensive and time-consuming to venture into faraway lands.

The Digital Estate has no rivers, mountains, or oceans to cross, only flickering points of presence, digital data on a screen. Approaching the World Wide Web as a great sprawling map that lies on top of the Internet allows any company to find international and multinational opportunities, transfer and translate information, conduct conferences, and negotiate and transact business. With expectations of from a hundred million to a billion users by the year 2000, it is no wonder that Digital Estate companies are eagerly testing the international waters.[1]

Thinking beyond borders electronically makes it practical to pursue business opportunities that were formerly impossible. However, this kind of global thinking requires a radical rethink, not only of place or geographic barriers, but of the less tangible qualities of space as well, as people have been suggesting for years. Just as the Net collapses the significance of time by permitting simultaneous, instant access, it also collapses the significance of space and place. Without geographic barriers, it is easy to tap into markets, such as Russia or China, that were formerly inaccessible or accessible to only a few.

From this perspective, any company who sets up shop on the Net extends its reach globally just by doing so. Almost everyone on the Net has a story about a user from another part of the globe dropping by their Web site. For example, when the FBI published its Ten Most Wanted list on the Web as a matter of course, a user in Central America recognized a fugitive and notified local police, which led to an arrest. Global reach is an inherent part of a network like the Internet. The ability to aggregate characters, or digital data, on a global scale is another way that companies in the Digital Estate are tapping into international opportunities. Without the Net, this cannot be done.

INTRANATIONAL AGGREGATION

As more and more countries are networked, there will be growth and expansion of what I have named Intranational Aggregation (IA), or the business of creating a platform which others can join to execute transactions, provide services, or furnish information. Aggregation is a natural fit in an environment comprising only digital data. At the most basic level, everything on the Net represents some form of aggregation, since someone had to bring together a grouping of sites, services, content, or community.

Because the kinds of aggregation made possible by the Net are new and unique, the challenge rests in discovery. If a company can see the globe in terms of the millions of ways it can be divided into an interactive, internetworked world, it stands a better than average chance of becoming an intranational aggregator. On the Net, anything and anyone can be aggregated, including suppliers, manufacturers, and even customers. IA extends that potential, so that a company can aggregate all over the world.

IA is in the early stages of development. But as new technologies and markets emerge, the aggregators force existing businesses to rethink their need and use of information, which can affect the kinds of products and services these companies produce. Unlike the landlord of even a virtual mall, IA creates value by devising new ways of using information rather than creating value through proximity. IA provides the necessary context for the corralled content. Here are some examples of companies that see the opportunities for intranational aggregation created by the Net:

- Effect Inc. in Tokyo set up virtual companies through its Web site to support venture business people. The company solicited people outside the group to join those virtual companies. Among its startups was Harika, one of the largest gift shops on the Internet. Harika features nearly 8,000 items, including everything from furniture and daily necessities to food. On its Worldeye site, the company targets the sale of used cars and makes hotel reservations.

- In China, James Chu, a U.S.-trained computer scientist, provides a network to enable users to set up their own home pages, trade information, draw on databases from around the world, and visit Web pages to which gatekeepers provide access. The China Internet Corp. rolls out a network of Web sites for 40 industrial cities in China. Content includes a wide range of products from auto parts to towels with a complete catalog of Chinese laws about trade and export, a translation service, and news. The virtual platform provided by the China Internet Corp. also has the potential to increase trade across the country, as more cities use the network and increase the total knowledge base. A client company has global reach instantly.

- A Maryland Internet design firm named EIN tapped into the international market by launching Central Europe Online Navigator and Russian Online Navigator, two English-language, advertising-supported Web sites. The sites were produced by the European Information Network, which is affiliated with and receives technical and financial support from Isis Interactive, Inc. When Central Europe Online (CEO) debuted, it featured business, political, travel, and financial information, in addition to Yellow Pages and classified advertising from Budvar, the German brewer of Budweiser, and European financial and travel groups. Content includes daily news updates about events in Poland, Hungary, Slovakia, the Czech Republic, and other countries in the region. Seventy percent of CEO users are from the United States. The company positioned itself as one of the new breed of intermediary or broker, a growing role in the Digital Estate.

- The Talent Network, aimed at production services professionals, created a global platform for finding technical, performing, and modeling talent. Clients create home pages and presentations using the Talent Network's facilities for nominal fees. The site gives its members international exposure. Production professionals can post notices and search the talent database by location, geographic region, agency, manager, or an identification code.

- The U.S.-based PlumbNet is a free resource open to plumbers, plumbing engineers, plumbing designers, architects, interior designers, and homeowners. In addition to its informational services, including plumbing and product news, regulatory codes, bulletin board discussion, and online expert advice, PlumbNet positions itself as a platform for plumbing-related professionals to build their online presence. The company offers advertising and packaged content, as well as online ordering facilities. While initially concentrating its efforts in the United States, PlumbNet is looking to expand its customer base internationally so that plumbing professionals all over the world can share information and resources.

These companies and others like them are breaking down geographic barriers and creating new value for the use and distribution of information. Aggregation, whether international or the most local, is inevitable in a virtual world with no geographic impediments, which in turn produces an overabundance of data and services. IA will continue to provide opportunities for the aggregators with the vision to see them. In the Digital Estate, the aggregator has a lead over the aggregated.

GLOBAL REACH

IA transforms the elusive barriers created by virtual space. The more tangible benefits of working in an internetworked world, however, are the hundreds of millions of potential consumers who will be connecting to the Net for an endless variety of reasons. Volume and variety should be incentive enough for companies hoping to extend their global reach in a digital world.

Once a product is conceived and launched on the Net, it is accessible anywhere, giving companies opportunities to extend their reach and potential customer base instantaneously. Even language barriers have been challenged. Though the language on the Net is predominantly English, Internet-focused language-translation services translate and un-Americanize companies' Web activities to target a country or language. Japanese companies, in particular, grasped the multinational Net concept early. Japanese companies routinely provide options for either Japanese or English versions of the site, which can be transposed at the click of a button.

THE PAPERLESS NEWSPAPER

In the heart of downtown Tokyo, four levels below street level, 400 multiton rolls of newsprint are perfectly aligned in columns and rows for as far as you can see.[2] This million dollars worth of paper will be gone in a few hours, as just part of the daily press run of *Asahi Shimbun,* Japan's second largest newspaper. The paper blankets the country with more than 8 million copies of its morning edition and almost 4.5 million copies of the evening edition every day, roughly 12 times the distribution of America's largest newspapers. The room reeks of the smell of ink, and the workers all wear dark blue uniforms and hats.

The two floors above house massive platemaking equipment to ready the plates for the presses, and a complex series of conveyor belts and folding machinery to convert the printed pages into finished, deliverable newspapers. For every tree that has to be chopped down to supply the presses' insatiable hunger for more paper, the newspaper company plants another tree to secure its long-term future. In the bowels of the building, outside a large room filled with mainframe computers, 14 dumb terminals serve as the umbilical cord connected to track the progress of the 32 rotary press units spinning at blinding speed and ear-deafening thunder. There, Mitsuo Deguchi, Deputy Manager of the Engineering Department, is understandably very proud of his large staff's daily production miracle.

Meanwhile, across the way, several floors above street level, the company is planning a different kind of future, one with sunshine and high-tech surroundings. A 13-member team of techno-journalists, led by 28-year-old Ohmae Jun-ichi, Manager of the Planning and Development Department, sits quietly in front of personal computers creating the electronic version of virtually everything downstairs with a difference. When these journalists hit a button on their PCs, the information they have compiled, crafted, and assembled is distributed instantaneously around the world on the World Wide Web, in both Japanese and English. And they don't have to cut down any trees to do it.

In April 1995, *Asahi Shimbun* formed an Electronic Media and Broadcasting Division to take advantage of anticipated technologies that allow for the easy manipulation of text, sound, and still and moving images. News is sent by computer on the Net, to electronic sign-boards on streets and aboard bullet trains, as well as to other computer networks. The information is also carried on news broadcasts of AM and FM radio stations. Also in the works is a massive database that has accumulated more than 80 years of text, pictures, and teletext, which will be accessible to anyone with a PC. "We cannot survive in a new area with the print arena alone," says Board Director Makoto Yasaka. "We have a 15-year vision, a long term vision, to coexist with the Net community. In the future, a single company cannot stand alone." The board members may not necessarily understand the details of virtual thinking, but they have the vision to realize that it is the future. They astutely identified the people most able to lead the charge, then put *them* in charge.

THE TOWERLESS RADIO STATION

Asahi Shimbun is a good example of how a very well established company is protecting its future by expanding its global reach. However, in the Digital Estate, a company doesn't have to be the second largest paper in Japan—or even the smallest paper in its hometown—to reach a global audience. New technologies will make such opportunities available at low enough cost that almost anyone can take advantage of them.

One such technology, a basic regeneration of the first wired revolution of this century, involves the transmission of live audio webcasts over the Net, allowing at least AM radio sound quality through normal PC speakers anywhere in the world. Progressive Networks introduced RealAudio data compression and decompression, allowing audio content to be delivered in near real-time. Millions of consumers have downloaded the RealAudio player from the Internet to their desktops, and hundreds of Web sites offer RealAudio content, including CBS, National Public Radio, and Hearst Magazines.

There are no traditional radio station costs, such as those for high transmission towers, not to mention the lack of oversight by the Federal Communications Commission. The technology lifted the geographic constraints of traditional radio signals, and a handful of Net radio pioneers filled the Net-waves. Their mission: to be the new networks.

- Dallas-based AudioNet, with live webcasts from the Superbowl, the NCAA Final Four games, and the National Hockey League, simulcasts the signals of 25 traditional radio systems nationwide as part of its Web-based enterprise, Net.Radio. AudioNet reached an agreement with the American Society of Composers, Authors, and Publishers (ASCAP), clearing the way for playing music on the Internet. The agreement allows Net.Radio to play music clips while protecting the copyrights of the music business and artistic communities. Besides music, the format focused on Internet news and provided a concert database that users could search by genre, band, and location.

- After broadcasting over the Net for only one month, "station" owner Scott Bourne in Minneapolis was offered seven figures to sell his company. Recent radio licenses in Minneapolis had sold for $22 million, while Bourne got up and running with $250,000, and, because he transmitted over the Net, his reach was instantaneously global. His e-mail hit 2,000 a day from places including Australia, Europe, and Sri Lanka. Program content includes American rock, classical music, concert information, music news, and promotional information. The sound quality isn't optimum, but listeners around the world appreciated the fact that they could even receive this sound and information, in real time, from a tiny station in Minneapolis.

THINKING BEYOND BUSINESS BORDERS

The global environment of the Web is an important new resource, not only for businesses, but also for individual users all over the world. The Net makes possible a service that is unique to this medium and without historical precedent. The Internet can connect people from all over the globe for a moment, an hour, a day in celebration or commemoration of a single event. This ability to aggregate people certainly holds commercial potential in, say, the case of a real-time broadcast of a rock concert, a football game, the CEO's speech, or a shareholders' meeting.

More than a commercial enterprise, the Internet is also a community, or rather millions of communities, filled with ordinary people whose ordinary lives have an extraordinary impact on the nature of the Net. In fact, there would be no Net without them. Business and government must work together to bring about mass connectivity through the adoption of standards and the creation of working commercial practices. But it is equally important to develop an infrastructure than ensures that the Net will remain an environment that all of those potential consumers will want to come to. There's no place like home and the Net is the digital home to the world. It is to everyone's advantage to support the growth and development of the personal aspects of Net life, as well as the commercial ones. Here are some examples of how some companies are using the Net for something more than profit:

- TerraQuest, a joint partnership of Mountain Travel Sobek and WorldTravel Partners, takes another approach to bypassing the limitations of time and space by updating the concept of the armchair traveler. These mouse-click travel adventures take full advantage of the interactive nature of the Net. The maiden voyage of TerraQuest followed the crew of the Livonia on its voyage from Ushuaia, Argentina, across Drake's Passage, into the mysterious world of Antarctica. More than 200,000 enthusiasts logged in for daily chats and live satellite uplinks for the two-week trip. The site also features interactive maps, videos, historical and scientific information, and a classroom workbook that gives "classroom correspondents" the opportunity to share and collaborate on educational projects.

- 24 Hours in Cyberspace: Drawings from the Digital Cave featured photographs digitally delivered from the mountains of Nepal to the monuments of Washington, D.C. The project represented the next logical step in the popular Day in the Life photography series by Rick Smolan. This time the scope was A Day in the Life of the World. One month later, more than 200 high-tech companies helped wire all 13,000 schools in California to connect five classrooms and their libraries to the Internet for Net Day.

- The New York Times created an interactive, multimedia photojournalism project to chronicle the end of the war in Bosnia. It featured an electronic gallery of more than 150 images by renowned photojournalist Gilles Peress and a month-long world-wide discussion on war and peace in former Yugoslavia. The *Times* ran the global discussions, and IBM donated technology so that terminals could be installed at the United Nations, the Hague, and Sarajevo University.

- On a lighter note, could it be that Fujitsu, Japan's largest computer company, is moving into the wedding business? Virtual events offer interesting possibilities for the future. Take the Valentine's Day nuptials of Joseph Perling and Victoria Vaughn. From his laptop at Venice Beach, the groom married his bride who was logged on from nearby Hollywood. The service was presided over by the Reverend John Perling, the groom's father, from his Beverly Hills church. As friends logged in from around the country, the couple assumed online personas and exchanged lawful vows in a virtual chapel in CompuServe's Worlds-Away community. The site, among the 20 most popular forums on CompuServe, is owned and operated by Fujitsu.

The Globe at Your Fingertips

Global thinking is an exciting and sometimes overwhelming prospect, with its limitless opportunities. Learning to see beyond geographic borders that have determined and influenced so much of human history is a valuable achievement.

The key to thinking globally is the ability to boldly imagine, as does *Asahi Shimbun*, making your product instantly available to hundreds of millions of people around the world every day. Companies that see the opportunity can move forward and create or aggregate just the right products and services to compete internationally.

Countries from India to Singapore are committing billions of dollars in joint industry/government partnerships to build a world-wide infrastructure for mass connectivity. The only analogy that even comes close to highlighting the level of this commitment is the rise of the military industrial complexes around the world during the course of the twentieth century. In the twenty-first century, strong telecommunications will be the weapon in the defense of a region's economic security. The new generals of the digital economy are the leaders of the Digital Estate. Armed with bits rather than bullets, these companies are finding that, in the borderless regions of cyberspace, aggregation is more effective than aggression. Global connectivity opens every connected border to an international pool of opportunity.

THE DIGITAL PUSH/PULL

Shouting on the Internet is considered impolite, even rude. It is one of the first rules of Netiquette that newcomers to the online world are likely to encounter. SHOUTING online is indicated by typing in all capital letters and is reserved as a textual display of emotion. Frequent and careless shouting results in retaliation from other users. The same general principle holds true for marketers. Commercial messages blasted at consumers just won't work in this environment. The audience has too much control.

On television, it takes high-speed action and catchy jingles to capture a couch potato's attention. On billboards, it takes quick messages and appealing images to grab the eye of passers-by. In magazines, newspapers, and radio, it takes a combination of high-impact messages with a clear value proposition to reach an audience quick to turn the page or flip the dial. In each of these cases, the consumer is the passive recipient of the message. That is, of course, if they even stop long enough to get the message. In the best case, consumers remember the message when it is time to go to the supermarket, buy a new car, or purchase home insurance. In the worst case, the message never registers at all. The effectiveness of this model, which pushes the message onto consumers whether they want it or not, is achieved by reaching a saturation point that transforms the message into brand recognition and that might pay off at the check-out counter.

This kind of pushing doesn't work in the Digital Estate. The Net is not only a medium of communication, but also an environment: a home, a neighborhood, a city, a mall, an adventure. It is whatever the user needs and desires it to be. Unwelcome intrusions are not tolerated because they don't have to be.

More importantly, intrusive messages don't work because the Web is inherently a pull medium. The interactive nature of the environment relegates message control to end users. On the Net, consumers themselves search for content along which a marketing message might ride. Consumers are in the driver's seat. To carry the analogy further, the consumers can easily turn off the main information highway down a road that is of personal interest. In the traditional marketplace, such detours are too isolated to be of much value to marketers looking for masses. After all, who puts billboards on small side roads?

On the Net, however, these interest avenues are often filled with consumers in the right frame of mind to receive helpful, service-oriented, targeted commercial messages. It is an opportunity not missed by the marketing mavens of the Digital Estate, who have learned that when "push-comes-to-shove," pulling is what works on the Net.

PULLCASTING

In the broadcast model, a company can say one thing, one way, one time, and reach millions of people with the same message. Examples of this include broadcast television, broadcast promotional brochures, broadcast discount sales, and broadcast price quotes. When Ronald MacDonald vouches for the value of a Happy Meal on TV, the intended audience is about as broad as it can get. It is targeted to children and to the adults (not just parents) who buy their meals. Everyone gets the same message. Although millions of people go online everyday, it is nearly impossible to reach large numbers of specific demographics at specific times.

The same holds true for narrowcast media, such as company-wide closed-circuit television conferences, direct mail to targeted audiences, special interest trade publications, and sales quotes narrowcast to the sales staff. As the term "narrowcast" implies, the field of recipients is narrow. Counterbalancing the decrease in volume is the advantage gained in targeting an audience predisposed for the messages.

Initially, the Internet was seen by some as a narrowcast medium because of its laser-like capabilities to reach very small audiences with specific, targeted messages. There is, however, an important difference. Unlike the audiences for broadcast and narrowcast, the online viewer can't be counted on to arrive at a location on time or be directed toward a specific subject at a given moment. The consumer, as the information recipient, controls and sometimes even creates the programming.

I call this pullcasting (see Fig. 6-1), which may at first seem like an oxymoron. After all, to pull is to haul in and to cast, in the context of marketing, is to throw outward. This might suggest that marketers should take a lesson from fishers and cast their nets out in order to pull consumers in, a strategy that is not altogether different from broad- and narrowcasting models. But leaders in the Digital Estate recognize that on the Net, the best way to angle one's perception is to take a 180-degree turn and look at the problem and solutions from the inside out. From this vantage point, the

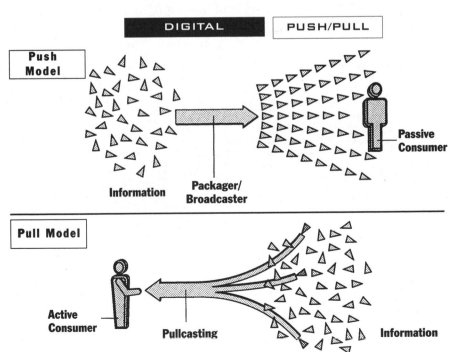

FIGURE 6.1

consumer does the pulling *and* the casting, and the "net" already exists. A company can provide incentive and a beckon to attract fishing consumers. A well-designed message, delivered at the right time and in the right circumstances, can entice consumers to pull it in of their own free will.

This last item is what makes doing business on the Net unique. While marketers devise and revise strategies to create compelling commercial messages to increase awareness or to drive sales, the user has to want to *pull* the information first. In pullcasting, consumers *pull* the information to their doors. What happens next depends on how well a company understands what its online customers want and how to provide it.

A comparison of broadcast, narrowcast, and pullcast shows that, while the reach and frequency in broadcast and narrowcast are more predictable and the potential volumes of consumers reached are higher, the effectiveness of pullcast exceeds the other approaches. (See Table 6-1.) This is because in an interactive environment, either consumers find a company's message, or the message finds them. Taking the scenario further, consumers initiate the interaction between the information provider and the information recipient: the seller and the buyer. The seller is presented with a unique opportunity to engage in a dialog with potential buyers at the very moment that they come looking for the information. Thus, the consumer *pulls* the information; the company doesn't have to push information out.

The inherent difficulty in pullcasting is that building a business is difficult when users must initiate the visit. Even the concept of a "visitor" to a company's information implies that that person is

Table 6-1.   Comparison Chart of Casting Models

	BROADCAST (TELEVISION)	NARROWCAST (CLOSED-CIRCUIT TV)	PULLCAST (THE INTERNET)
Consumer	Passive	Active	Interactive
Commercial message	Mass market	Targeted	Very targeted
Driver	Broadcaster	Narrowcaster	Viewer/user
Reach	High volume	Medium volume	Low volume
Frequency	High	Medium	Low
Predictability	High	Medium	High

just passing through, and may or may not ever return. This is the ultimate challenge of pullcasting. If a company fails to deliver useful ads, commercials, promotions, and other offerings to satisfy the specific consumer's needs during the visit, the consumer can vanish at the click of a button.

'OH, NO! HE'S GOT CLICKITIS!'

In the early days of cable TV and paid programming, broadcasters such as CNN, ESPN, HBO and Showtime would measure and predict audience viewing and usage. Then along came the VCR, and people could rent and watch movies, even if they couldn't set the blinking "12:00" on the front. Consumers eventually started to tape programs from TV and watched them later, creating the *time-shifting* phenomenon. People, in effect, created their own packages of shows, to watch when they wanted. They created their own channels, based on a smorgasbord of broadcast and cable offerings. Zapping, or the tendency to fast-forward, posed a serious threat to companies whose million-dollar commercials could be skipped by the touch of a button.

On the Net, a similar phenomenon occurs, but to a much greater extent. A fundamental part of the experience of searching and surfing online is zapping, which is fast-forwarding through sites even as a page is uploading to the screen. Unlike its counterpart in television, this activity is actually central to the operation of being online. For example, users go online and log in. Up comes the browser. The *splash,* or front page, contains various options. Users may search or check a preselected list of What's Cool or What's New. They may want to send mail, access a newsgroup, or go directly to a bookmarked URL. Any action requires that the user click and leave this home page. And so it goes at any site anywhere on the Web. Click, click, click.

Unlike the commercial breaks recorded on a VCR tape, which run their course whether or not the viewer zaps through them, a page on the Net is there until the user clicks away from it. The mouse (or the keyboard for die-hards) is essentially the user's only form of transportation. This fact has led to the development of another phenomenon I've named *clickitis* (pronounced "click-eye-tis"), or clicking as a matter of habit. With so many options to choose from, consumers on the Net rarely stay in any one place for long. If a site is interesting but tangential to the user at the moment, it may be bookmarked. If the site takes too long to load, a user clicks out. If the top of the page that is loading has an inviting linking banner, the user might click straight onto it, not waiting to see what the rest of the page, much less the site, has to offer.

This presents marketers with a dual challenge. Not only do they have to worry about getting customers to their sites; they also have to devise strategies for keeping them there long enough to do some good. The beauty of effective pullcasting is that it offers a solution to both problems. The burden that this remedy places on marketers is the need both to attract attention and to make sure that, once customers arrive at the door, they are immediately ushered into the site and given plenty of reasons to stay there. Pullcasting, at its best, does precisely this.

The efforts of Netcentric companies, whose core business is developing the technologies that move people and information around in cyberspace, have affected the evolution of pullcasting on the Net.

LESSONS FROM THE FRONT LINE

Many people wouldn't remember to pay their bills if the bills didn't come in the mail each month. Those monthly pieces of mail start the chain of events. The bills come, go into a pile, and are sorted. At check-writing time the checks are written and put into envelopes, which are stamped and mailed. Many consumers approach the Net the same way. They don't remember to go regularly to places that they know they either should go or wanted to go, but forgot or didn't get around to it.

In 1994, when the bi-weekly Internet trade newspaper *Interactive Age* was launched, it also launched several daily news services on the World Wide Web. These services were free to anyone who visited the *Interactive Age* home page, which was among the most visited of parent company CMP's 13 technology publications. The newspaper received countless comments from readers who said they liked the daily news services but didn't remember to go to the site every day. Based on these requests, *Interactive Age* launched an e-mail version of the daily services and offered subscriptions for $100 per year. Hundreds of people subscribed almost overnight. Paying to have the information delivered was easier for consumers than remembering to search in the course of a busy day, even though they could have *pulled* the information out of the Net for free. Most people still went to the location to see the stories daily, but for many the convenience of delivery to the desktop was appealing enough to pay a premium.

ON WITH THE ONLINE/OFFLINE AGENTS

Leaders in the Digital Estate recognized the potential of delivery services early, and Internet startup companies formed to create new delivery mechanisms called Online/Offline Agents to solve the problem. Also called *push agents,* these electronic agents *pull* selective information from the World Wide Web gathered on a time frame selected by the consumer and deliver the information to the consumer's desktop in the background, maybe even while the consumer is sleeping. When the daily electronic information arrives, a message may flash on the screen to notify the recipient. When the desktop hasn't been used for a number of minutes, a screensaver is initiated, which may include friendly prompts for all this information, as well as a few advertising messages or logos from companies that pay to ride along with the agent.

Companies offer variations of online/offline agents. Some, such as Freeloader, are loaded with menus from various content providers. Others will target employees at large and small companies at work, through corporate Intranets, or internal networks. Employees have access not only to specific electronic publications they need for their jobs, but also to companywide messages such as news, sales information, and job training. Important messages from headquarters can be up-to-date on every employee's PC anywhere in the world. Employees are able to *pull* any information related to their company and their jobs from the company database, all translated into friendly-looking HTML screens. At the same time, company executives and services can *push* relevant messages to employees and have them pop up on employees' screensavers.

An added bonus of online/offline agents is that while the world awaits higher bandwidth to increase the multimedia capabilities of the Web, this interim technology allows large data streams to be sent during users' downtime and stored on their PCs so that the information is readily available, instantaneously. This effectively creates the illusion of full bandwidth, providing capabilities of rich video and sound.

"JUST BROWSING"

Push agents represent one way a company might deliver information, circumventing the *pull* nature of the medium. However, by far the most popular method for people to obtain their information and entertainment is logging directly onto the World Wide Web and *pulling* information through their browser or navigator. This made navigators hot property for advertisers looking to cash in on users who had not yet contracted clickitis. Recognizing the power of first contact, the navigation companies build their own content, including site reviews, news updates, and beta versions of their upgrades.

Netscape, not surprisingly, leads the pack as it positions itself to become an Internet client. In addition to the standard features, Netscape added Internet phone capability, whiteboard communications, and collaboration tools. The upshot of all these add-ons is that browsers are and will continue to be the primary launchpad for the Net. They are central to the quality of the consumer's online experience, which creates an intensive level of brand loyalty. Navigators or browsers are a user's home away from home.

The relationship between a user and a browser is important for several reasons. Popular navigators such as Netscape and Microsoft's Internet Explorer never stop adding. They load up their sites with services and products, then pile on more. It is an interesting strategy to emulate. Customers find reason to stay longer and develop an affinity for the site.

To users, the browser is a family face to the Web. For merchants, the browser represents an opportunity to attract customers. The value of the navigation locations is the sheer volume of eager browsers that pass through their portals, making them essential components of Net life and of Net business.

The importance of these numbers rests in their potential as markets. Word spreads like lightning within the network. When Silicon Valley startup Excite launched its Web navigation agent, it did so without advertising or promotion. It created a superior product, which included computer-generated summaries of items found throughout the World Wide Web, as well as its own staff-written reviews of tens of thousands of sites. It allowed consumers to find stories based on the context of what they were looking for. This context-based searching capability was new in the Net environment. The company launched the product on the Web and let consumers find it. And find it they did. Within only six months of launch, it garnered almost 10 percent market share of all navigation agents on the Net. This group of young Stanford graduates understood the *pull* power of the Web.

NEGOTIATING THE DIGITAL PULL/PUSH

Not all companies doing business in an internetworked world are in the business of creating push/pull technologies. Nevertheless, companies in any business can both use these technologies to their advantage and learn from their experience with the art of the digital pull/push.

Madison Avenue was initially a bit perplexed about how to handle the Internet pull model. Advertisers first created banner advertising and sought to route traffic to their locations through the traffic of others. This led to banner or billboard advertising, where advertisements were scattered throughout mainly front pages of hundreds of Web sites. This strategy relied on traffic volume. The more traffic a Web site could claim, the better the chances that at least some of the visitors would click onto the banner advertisement adorning the site. Unlike broadcasting, however, the choice to view the ad was, in every sense of the word, in the hand of the user. Once tracking agents evolved to the point that they could accurately pinpoint the number of users who clicked onto an ad and measure to some extent the value of the experience, marketers began to recognize the need for a bold rethinking of how to communicate with online consumers.

This led to the idea that advertisers could create compelling content that would retain consumers at least long enough for an advertiser's message to be effective. The online consumer goes to a marketing site to access information or a service. An additional benefit to adding content and services to a site that might originally have been intended only as a marketing campaign is that the customer's interaction has a recursive effect on the company business. Customers are finding themselves increasingly performing tasks once relegated to in-house staffs, and thanking the company for the convenience to boot!

The Net is a powerful medium for information-based businesses that can reduce or eliminate the cost of gatekeepers, such as reservation clerks and customer services representatives. As an example, Hyatt creates a Web location that allows consumers looking for a vacation spot to check out all the Hyatt properties, with highlights of the best deals, with detailed photography and room layouts. The searching consumers *pull* all the necessary information from Hyatt, which offloads the reservation agent function directly to the consumer. The challenge for Hyatt is to *push* to the potential traveler the message that Hyatt has a special deal this month, or that there is a new Hotel grand opening in one month, or that there are bonus Gold Passport points for stays at certain hotels in November. Hyatt, or any other hotel, might address this issue in two ways: It could either *push* the content to the potential traveler or *push* the potential traveler to the information, what I refer to as "herding" in the Digital Estate. Companies can create and promote contests and rewards through heavy advertising and corral large numbers of people at their locations. Sometimes this is accomplished by the large-scale aggregation of well-known products.

This is a strategy favored by media companies. CMP's TechWeb, ZiffDavis' ZDNet, and Time-Warner's Pathfinder have gathered their many publications around a common site, giving users access to a vast array of content. Pathfinder is home to *Time, Sports Illustrated, People, Life, AsiaWeek, Fortune, The Progressive Farmer, HBO,* and *Entertainment Weekly,* to name just a few. Like the commercial online services, such as America Online or CompuServe,

Pathfinder is a large-scale content aggregator with an eye to building online communities among its users. While most of the content is derived from the company's print publications, it also offers content from other media companies. Herding in this context is not pushing consumers toward a particular product or service, as was the case with Hyatt. It is rather a way to corral visitors, offering them so much internal content that they have little incentive to click out of the site.

SEVEN APPROACHES TO THE DIGITAL PUSH/PULL

To be captured by the information- and entertainment-hungry consumer, companies in the Digital Estate must cultivate new approaches to the digital push/pull. There are seven, including:

- *Create Valuable or Appealing Content.* Historically the province of traditional content providers, the Net opens the door for any company to create compelling content that surfing consumers will value. Kaplan Educational Centers, for example, promoted its testing preparation services with a sense of humor. Interactive games included The Hot Seat, a mock interview, and The Amazing College Simulator that separates the party animals from the pocket protectors. The heart of the site is information and ordering for the test materials. Nevertheless, Kaplan went the extra mile to provide its customers, most of whom are probably not thrilled at the prospect of taking a major exam, with loads of relevant information, games, a chat and bulletin board, and a Career & Classifieds Center.

- *Create Valuable Service.* Free is a hard price to beat. Fortunately for users, on the Net it is one of the most popular strategies for attracting consumers. Two companies offering free e-mail software to consumers hope to cash in on the advertising banners attached to the post. Freemark, a small company in Cambridge, Massachusetts, partnered with Citibank to comarket with a range of companies, including Radio Shack and NetGuide. Juno, owned by investment company D.E. Shaw & Co., tackled the market by spending $20 million on a national ad campaign. The impetus behind the efforts of both companies was the recognition that, while millions of users had modems, only a small percentage of them were going online. By making their e-mail systems free, the start-ups hoped to be just the adapter needed to hook those modems into phone lines.

- *Heavily Promote to Drive Mass Traffic to a Site.* Even the most enthusiastic member of the Digital Estate laughs sometimes at the explosion of URL ads. They are tagged onto ads on television, on the radio, in newspapers, and in magazines. No doubt they will eventually show up as urban graffiti. But this form of promotion is a very powerful and simple way to give the consumers what they need to pull in a corporate site. Similarly, some of the most popular sites, such as CNET and Pathfinder, also heavily promote themselves with banner ads online, as well as by advertising in traditional venues.

- *Selectively Target to Drive a Specific Audience to a Site.* Companies can determine where on the Net their target audience is likely to be found. If a company is seeking to market sports shoes, it can promote its wares on a sports-oriented Web location, such as ESPN SportsZone or the NBA All Star game site. If high-volume sites are too expensive, companies can be more creative. For example, a site called Veggies Unite, an online guide to vegetarianism, is an ideal site for health food mail order companies to post their banners. The Pleadies Network or Women's Wire, both of which address the vanishing distinction between a woman's professional and personal interests, might make perfect sites for SOHO (Small Office Home Office) companies to advertise.

- *Create Community.* Companies can create communities of interest in which like-minded or like-interested individuals can gather. This increases brand affinity and allows consumers to be pulled into the company's environment, although a company should take great pains to assure that the community is run by its members. Zima created a community of interest and created a loyal following though its Web site, where hip twenty-somethings join Tribe Z and receive lots of cool digital gifts.

- *Reward the Consumer.* If nothing else, companies can simply reward consumers for a visit. Contests and coupons are the most tried and true approaches on the Net. Because the customer actually does the pulling, companies must offer some kind of incentive. American Airlines offered chances to win first-class tickets for two to desirable destinations, while I/PRO bartered consumer information for cash prizes and vacation giveaways. The practice became so common that online consumers take it for granted. Advertisers that give nothing back, either in terms of incentives or services, will feel the chill.

- *Ride with a Push Agent.* As the number of push agents grows, so will the opportunity for marketing messages to ride along with them. These smart agents can display ad messages as screen savers or insert them on a company's newest product or sale. Saturn, Prodigy, Fidelity Investments, and Twentieth Century Fox hooked up with Pointcast so their advertising messages would be rotated on screen savers downloaded to consumers' desktops. Another example of effective piggybacking is MapQuest, a free interactive mapping service that accepts sponsorships. A user traveling from Denver to Los Angeles might look for all available gas stations en route. When they search, a logo comes up with their search results.

NET BONDING

Companies have been trying for years to create services to build and enhance relationships with their customers. Can the Internet help? Yes! The Internet is a service-oriented medium, with inherent one-to-one characteristics, that can provide companies with interactive strategies that range from marketing and promotion through product sales.

Some may look at the Net as a vast, impersonal collection of unrelated information, with thousands of companies vying for consumers' dollars. While the Net may seem endless when searching for specific needs, many companies in the Digital Estate have found ways to serve individuals so that they not only return, but also develop an affinity for providers of the service. Just as Nordstrom's gained its reputation for the ultimate in value-added service, making the shopping experience *feel* good, leaders of the Digital Estate are creating similar relationship models in cyberspace. They find that not only do consumers use the service, but they even feel good about it.

In its early incarnations, the World Wide Web contained basic information provided by companies. Consumers who searched for Delta Airlines, for example, expected to find information about the airline company, maybe its planes, and the names of the corporate officers. They expected to find basic information on virtually all serious companies with a quick Internet search. Advertising was more promotional in nature.

In the next iteration, consumers will search for service and *expect* to obtain what they will consider basic services. They will *expect* to be able to check their itinerary through any airline, directly book travel anywhere, make their dinner and concert reservations after viewing available seating, and get price quotes on appliances, cars, and clothes, and execute transactions with any businesses they choose. Those not providing the service will not be considered options, since they won't even participate in the electronic selection process.

Participation enables companies to redefine relationships with their customers and, through some simple techniques, to improve how they are perceived. Companies have found ways to get closer to their customers, to bond with them. Business through the Net is not about overwhelming customers with masses of data, but about providing highly customized and valuable knowledge or service to individuals. Several companies have learned that they can collect regular fees for these services, while keeping customers satisfied.

SERVICE, SERVICE, SERVICE

The Net offers several options for building relationships, especially when companies focus on increasing their service to their customers. When Federal Express and United Parcel Service allow customers into their databases to track their own packages, the service actually empowers customers. Other areas that companies in the Digital Estate use to strengthen customer relationships include providing customized areas of interest, such as family and household issues or business information.

FAMILY/HOUSEHOLD

In an internetworked world, consumers browse, shop, and purchase in new ways. The walking-the-aisle experience is supplemented or supplanted by surfing through thousands of aisles at high speed. In this environment, with digital money and unlimited product selection, consumers find companies competing among themselves and directly with manufacturers and suppliers. When consumers feel that a company on the Net serves them, they return.

No longer constrained by corporate decisions to carry or not to carry certain products, consumers can find anything on the Net and obtain it directly. Companies can focus on building relationships by offering services unique to the environment. They can take advantage of the opportunity to connect and interact, one-on-

one, with consumers. Not only does the Net create the means for establishing this kind of relationship between businesses and consumers: A company's success depends on it.

There is not much that is not already available through the Net: lobsters, real estate, vacation packages, and coupons, with the volume of products and services growing daily. Service can always be increased, because the medium allows businesses to know who a customer is, what that customer wants, and when that customer wants it.

HAPPY GROCERY SHOPPERS

The emerging and major players in the world of electronic groceries serve as a model of how one industry is learning to embrace new service options to keep the customer satisfied. The food industry might not be expected to blaze a trail through cyberspace, given the high priority placed on the tactile nature of grocery shopping. Such is the case with the online grocery service Peapod. Based in Evanston, Illinois with a branch operation in the San Francisco area, Peapod is the brainchild of the Parkinson brothers, Andrew and Thomas, who saw a statistic that 60 percent of all shoppers didn't want to shop in grocery stores.

The brothers, both of whom had marketing backgrounds and one of whom already owned his own software company, recognized the potential for electronic grocery shopping and set out to attract the 60 percenters. In 1991 they teamed up with a Jewel Food Store in northern Chicago and later with Safeway in San Francisco. Within a few years, Peapod topped 10,000 customers in the Chicago area and 3,000 in San Francisco. Peapod is taking its growth in stride, building an intensely loyal following in local markets by keeping the quality of its service high. The electronic grocery enterprise has also attracted the attention of investors including Ameritech, The Tribune Company, and the Providence Journal.

Peapod, as previously mentioned, has a following, boasting a retention rate of nearly 80 percent, almost 80 percent of whom are women. The attraction is clear: Electronic grocery shopping is a service worth paying for if it can save valuable time. The evidence is not only that customers keep coming back but that they do so at some expense.

Peapod is not exactly cheap. The company originally charged a start-up fee of $29.95, which ultimately was eliminated. But the monthly fee of $4.95, and a charge of $6.95 per order plus 5 percent of the total purchase remain. It seems, however, that Peapod can actually save shoppers money as well as time. Customers shopping online are less likely to succumb to impulse buying. They also are more likely to use coupons. Peapod distributes some electronic coupons, but it also honors coupons that its customers have collected.

Individuals using Peapod's Web site can perform a variety of options. They can:

- Access the databases and catalogs of designated supermarkets.
- Comparison shop.
- Access information about nutrition.
- Sort items by various criteria, such as price, price/unit, total calories, fat, protein, carbohydrates, cholesterol, and sodium.
- Even check to see if an item is Kosher. Searches can be directed to find brand names or product types.

The software also allows customers to give specific instructions, such as "green bananas only." Shoppers can subtotal at any time and check the items they have put into their electronic shopping carts. The software also permits users to save lists that can then be reordered—a handy and time-saving idea for annual Thanksgiving dinners or weekly staples. To order, a user clicks the button and chooses a delivery time within a 90-minute delivery slot. A 30-minute delivery period is available for an additional fee. Payments can be made with checks, by credit cards, or through Peapod's electronic payment option.

But who thumps the melons and smells the meat? The Peapod strategy is to assure the quality of the items delivered by training a staff of professional shoppers. While this model creates an expensive overhead for the company, it also allows Peapod more flexibility and control over the operation. As the business expands, personal grocery shoppers might pick up items from specialty shops and farmer's markets, as well as from supermarkets. But with 4 percent of the $400-billion grocery and drug shopping market going online by the year 2000 according to company estimates, Peapod is willing to do whatever it takes to service those consumers.

Not surprisingly, Peapod is not alone. Here's a sampling of other shopping service business models:

- *Shoppers Express.* Shoppers Express, a Bethesda, Maryland company that has tested the online waters through partnerships with both America Online and Time Warner's Full Service Network, created a Net grocery shopping service called ShoppingLink. Customers access the database of local partner grocery stores and shop in a fashion similar to that of Peapod. Delivery, however, is a flat fee of $9.95 per order, regardless of the dollar amount of the purchase. Another difference is the use of surrogate shoppers provided by the grocery store rather than a staff maintained by the service. ShoppingLink may position itself as a local content provider for cable and phone companies as part of Internet access value-added services.

- *Kroger.* Third-party shopping services may run up against stiff competition if major supermarkets start offering their own services. Kroger in Columbus, Ohio is doing just that. It offers free access through the Net for customers who can browse through the company's catalog or search through an online database. Kroger uses in-store employees to shop and deliver orders to customers. Delivery fees are $10 for purchases of up to $100 and 10 percent of the total order for purchases over $100. Pick-up service is $5 or 5 percent of orders over $100.

- *Smart-Food Co-op.* This company offers free access and free delivery, plus substantial food discounts. Perhaps more important, is the profile of SFC's initial market: residents and nearby high-tech neighborhoods of MIT. Today's MIT student provides an interesting glimpse into the future. Consumers accustomed to a certain level of service take its availability for granted. SFC, in fact, is not really a new idea at MIT. It was started in 1980 as a student co-op arrangement among ZBT, the French House, and members of Ashdown House to save time and money by buying in bulk. When the original members graduated, however, the co-op fizzled. Ten years later, the idea was revived and membership expanded. The move to the Web was part of that expansion. The SFC also uses the Net to create channels of communication by encouraging members to exchange thoughts and recipes. SFC shoppers browse by alphabetical order, category, and single-word entries. SFC orders items wholesale and has made deals with area stores. SFC also passes along savings achieved by purchasing special sale items. Because it is a co-op, service is the only incentive for maintaining the operation. Profit is not a factor. However, SFC is an interesting twist in the current trend among online grocery services. Such grocery shopping services may well become as ubiquitous on college campuses as the cafeteria. A derivation of targeting a very specific market might be gated communities, such as retirement villages, which might offer electronic shopping as a free service to entice elderly clients.

- *Great Food Online.* Yet another approach to electronic grocery shopping is the specialty or gourmet strategy used by a small startup in the Pacific Northwest. Great Food Online is a labor of love for Ben and Donna Nourse, a couple whose interests include technology and fabulous food. From a home page on the Web, customers can buy direct from suppliers. Great Food Online might, for instance, feature a recipe using pesto. With a quick click on the product name in the recipe, the user is transported to the supplier's site. All items that are available through Great Foods are hotlinked to the supplier so that users can easily order the specialty items. Shipping is processed within 24 hours, but it may take several days for delivery depending on the kind of mail options a user chooses. Although the selections currently offered by the company are limited, this model for specialty shopping demonstrates how the Web can be used to create a service that may otherwise be unavailable to most people. Without much outlay or expense, Great Food Online can successfully link small, local producers to a national and international market.

- *Lobsters on the Net.* The obvious extension of this kind of thinking is the direct purchase by consumers from producers/suppliers, direct marketing in its purest form. On the Net, even fresh lobster is only a click or two away. In fact, there are several lobster sites on the Web, including Lobster Direct, Maine Lobster Direct, Shore to Door, Port Lobster, New England Live Lobster, and the Lobster House. Most started as one-page ads with an invitation to call an 800 number to place an order for overnight delivery, although some moved to online ordering. Some of the companies are experimenting to enhance their service. Lobster Direct has recipes, a monthly e-mail newsletter, lobster tips, environmental information, and a bulletin board. By utilizing the interactive nature of the Net, the company creates more demand for its product. The monthly newsletter, while fun and informative, is also a not so subtle reminder that a fresh lobster is only 24 hours away. Customers can add their favorite recipes or exchange tips with one another, creating a community of common interest. Once a participant in such a community, the customer is likely to come back. Maine Lobster Direct provides content for its site in the form of recipes, lobster lore, tips, and special information. The company also includes an online discount coupon and ships through Federal Express to anywhere in the United States, as well as to Canada and to Japan. The Lobster House, a restaurant and popular tourist stop along the New Jersey shore that has been in operation since 1922, has its own fishing fleet and fish market that carries Norwegian salmon, Maryland crabmeat, and Alaskan halibut. The Lobster House also takes orders over the Net, featuring items that can be purchased, delivered overnight, and, if desired, precooked.

In addition to providing customers with a time-saving device, companies can create communities among consumers. Shore-to-door delivery is combined with the ability for a company to become a social part of a customer's life. This aspect makes shopping on the Net more like the old town square than the suburban mall. People shop and talk, share and spend. The value-added service of promoting these communities gives companies the opportunity to create successful relationships with their customers.

Shopping is not isolated to grocery and lobster stores. Spearheaded by Andersen Consulting, the Consumer Direct Cooperative is tracking 60 customers of a fax-based delivery service in the Boston area, trying to determine how shoppers function in a virtual environment. The members are Procter & Gamble, Coke, Gillette, Kraft, Nabisco, Ocean Spray, Ralston Purina, Sara Lee, and Smuckers.

DIGITAL COUPONS

Even the consumers who are willing to pay for a useful service are just as willing to save money. Coupons have long been a favorite marketing device because they allow customers to save money by simultaneously directing traffic straight to a product. Everybody wins. Coupons have been so successful that many consumers take them for granted. Coupons are everywhere: in-store coupon dispensers, newspaper supplements, coupon mailers, product packaging coupons, double daily coupons, and Wednesday bonus specials.

Coupons are alive and thriving on the Net. Money Mailer, which distributes paper coupons to more than 100 million households weekly, launched the Internet coupon called H.O.T. Coupons. The premise is simple: The online consumer goes to Money Mailer's Web site, types in his or her zip code, and identifies a product or service. If a coupon is available, the user prints it and uses it. The site features the company's entire database of millions of coupons for local, regional, and national products and services. Val-Pak Direct Marketing Systems is also exploring coupon distribution through the Web, and Advo, the successful Connecticut direct marketer, is aggressively moving to online, interactive coupons.

As electronic grocery shopping and services such as digital coupons become standards, they, like ATMs, can evolve from value-added services to necessities. The Net is particularly and uniquely suited for such a task because consumers themselves can participate in the marketing process. Coupon services are positioning themselves as useful service providers in an internetworked world. It is not difficult to make the leap from static coupons to coupons that adopt personal preference technologies which collate individual preferences with broader-based databases geared toward identifying potential purchase patterns. Leaders in the Digital Estate understand that the key to keeping consumers coming back is to engage them, to create innovative services today that will be the staples of tomorrow.

Also expanding is the range of coupon distribution. During the 1996 Summer Olympic Games, for instance, Reebok introduced a global coupon campaign targeting Asian markets in Taiwan, Korea, and Hong Kong. Cosponsored with V1, a prominent music and entertainment cable service in Asia, Reebok distributed coupons through its Web site for 20 percent off its products. The coupons could be redeemed with retailers in the designated countries, as well as at the company's store in Atlanta.

GETTING PERSONAL

The key to transforming marketing into service is the distance between consumers' interest in a product and their purchase of it. Less obvious is how to close the gap. Agents, inc. is one Digital Estate company that has found a way to bridge the gap with a product it calls Firefly. Derived from research at MIT focused on sorting e-mail, Firefly assigns its members an intelligent agent. The agent learn users likes and dislikes and provides them with personalized recommendations. Users can leverage their agent to find other people within the Firefly community who have shared their musical tastes and to whom they can communicate through real-time chat and one-to-one messaging. Comparing the consumer's musical interests to those who have similar tastes, the agent makes personalized recommendations on music and movies that the querying consumer might also like.

Firefly quickly established itself as a destination site for Internet users. Advertisers were able to construct targeted messages to these users based on several criteria, including entertainment preferences, age, gender, zip codes, country information, domain, computing platform, and browser type. Once the marketer determines the profile of the target consumer, the agent searches through multiple ad banners and delivers the appropriate ad to the user. In other words, Firefly's intelligent agent technology ensures that the right messages are delivered to the appropriate individuals. By not asking for users' names or addresses, Firefly guarantees the privacy and integrity of information about its user base.

Firefly users also review advertising banners according to how successful marketers have been in creatively targeting their messages. Consumers have the opportunity to rate each advertiser's message based on its relevance to them, as they would rate an album or movie on the Firefly site. This furnishes advertisers with both a quantitative and a qualitative measurement, a unique benefit not only for advertising on the Web but also for broadcast media as well. Says CEO Nick Grouf:

> The Web is a fundamental paradigm shift away from broadcasting. You can give each individual their own personal experience, and give each individual information about what they are interested in, from an advertising standpoint. Advertisers can come to us and they can say "I want this ad to go to a certain demographic, and then this ad to go to a different demographic" and the consumer receives ads that are relevant to them. The ad becomes an important piece of information. You can let a consumer *pull* an advertisement. In a car ad, the agent knows that safety and fuel efficiency matter to me so I get a tailored ad that addresses those concerns. Consumers are willing to share their information preferences and we have effectively become a matching service. Our users even created their own Firefly forum that meets once a month electronically, and we only participate if we're invited. One user in Amsterdam didn't like one part of an ad, so he set up his own home page and invited people to vote on whether that part of the ad should be eliminated. And since our users rate the ads, word would have gotten back to the advertiser as feedback (the consumers voted to keep the part of the ad). In our service, the data belongs to the consumer, we don't take names or addresses. Your agent goes out and meets with other agent, weights them and over time learns. We become a bank for people's preferences. People like their agents and their community.

The Agents, inc. technology is being licensed to many companies, so that they too can increase their service to their consumers, enhancing the relationship. Firefly attracted hundreds of thousands of registered users within months of launch. Agents, inc. has company in its dedication to strengthening relationships between buyers and sellers. Here is a sampling:

- *Amazon.com* keeps records of people's reading preferences, suggests books, and sends alerts by e-mail if there's something new by a desired author. It lists more than a million titles that can be purchased directly online. The company is almost totally virtual, acting as a wholesaler, with little inventory and overhead.

- *Individual, Inc.* is the licensee for an agent technology, developed at Cornell University, that filters, retrieves, and ranks information in order of importance for the user. The company creates a link between a large network of content providers and the unique interests of the customers. The company acts as a personal agent for its clients, actively working on their behalf to find otherwise inaccessible, but relevant, information. Its customized news products are created by an interactive, self-learning software agent that searches a broad spectrum of electronic wire services, newspapers, and trade periodicals to find the articles uniquely relevant to each client. Information selected by the agent for each subscriber is automatically fed into a custom-designed newsletter format, and then delivered via e-mail, through the Net, by fax, or onto enterprisewide groupware platforms such as Lotus Notes and Collabra Share.

REACHING THE NET-BASED BUSINESS CONSUMER

Service opportunities extend beyond personal and recreational interests in an internetworked world. The business consumer presents a large opportunity for providing useful services through the Net. Here are some examples:

- *Nets Inc.* is an electronic information and database marketing company specializing in business and industry in the United States and Canada. Founded in 1990 as Industry.Net, its stated goal is to bring buyers and sellers together in an interactive environment. The company developed 25 online services, and has business centers for more than 4,000 companies with information on 250,000 suppliers. Industry.Net grew more than 200 percent per year from startup and ultimately received an investment from AT&T. The annual buying power of the Nets Inc. member network exceeds $165 billion.

- *@griculture Online,* a venture of *Successful Farming* magazine, a publication of the Meredith Corp., was designed to reach out to producers, agribusinesses, experts, researchers, universities, and youth groups. The company targets subscription services, including one to provide interactive maps to go with a weather service.

- *American Airlines* provides all you'd expect from an in-person airline reservation agent, including fares after the traveler supplies the specific itinerary information and package deals. It also furnishes customer relationship building programs, including scheduled silent auctions on first-class tickets to various cities, with the proceeds going to charity. When it launched its access program not only to directly book flights, hotels, and car rentals, but even to change flight seating, it offered its interactive travel planning software first to its frequent flyers in advance of the general public.

- *Hyatt* not only provides details on every Hyatt Hotel in the world, but also gives room availability for travelers' specific dates. Reservations may be made online.

A business can develop fruitful relationships with Net-based consumers by offering services that would be impractical in another medium. Sears could hardly be expected to know that Agnes Theriault prefers brown to peach or that Ann Marie Nadeau wears jeans and never khakis. But on the Net, Sears can not only discover such preferences, but also take that discovery a step further. New technologies make it possible to anticipate and respond to the needs of individual customers.

TRANSFORMING SELLING INTO SERVICE

This ability to anticipate transforms selling into a service. As new intelligent agents find patterns as they sift through data, they can collect specified information, such as stock quotes or a newspaper, keep track of individual preferences, and deliver the information accordingly. Imagine an advertising strategy that can create specific content tailored to individual interest. Then imagine placing that ad in front of the consumer at just the moment it is needed. The commercial message is transformed into an information-rich, targeted, useful message: a *service* to the consumer.

While the Net provides the means for businesses to connect with their customers, contacting and keeping customers are not the same thing, especially in an environment designed for distractions. While new technologies can enhance and create new service options, quality service depends on the ability to identify a need and on the creativity to fulfill it. In the Digital Estate, interactive learning is the single best strategy that a company can employ when exploring this environment. Doing business on the Net is much more about learning how to learn, how to move, how to communicate, how to thrive. As companies close the gap between their customers' needs and their fulfillment, the quality of service can only improve. The higher the level of service, the better the company-customer relationship will be.

DO THAT VISION THING

In spite of the proliferation of corporate home pages on the Web, some, and maybe many, executives question the need to rush into this new environment, but they are doing it anyway. Unlike start-ups with no core business to consider, established companies tend to favor a conservative approach to new ideas that may turn out to be a fad rather than a true trend. One CEO, sure that having an interactive strategy is important, but unsure of exactly why, suggested the following analogy:

> Imagine a movie theater. The CEO of a Fortune 500 company buys a ticket and takes a seat for the show. Another company CEO sees the executive there, so he buys a ticket. The theater eventually fills and one executive goes for popcorn. Then another. Then another. Eventually, all have popcorn. So, here they all are, tickets paid, popcorn purchased, waiting for the word to come down. So they sit. And sit. And sit.

Joining the bandwagon is rarely a good strategic move if jumping on the wagon is a company's only motive. Unfortunately, many of the companies that established a presence on the Internet did so out of fear that they might be left behind. While fear of losing ground to a competitor is normal and healthy, fear unattended by a clear vision of a company's ultimate goals may just be a ticket into the wrong theater.

While no one can project with certainty the evolution of business on the Net, success is strongly in favor of companies that spend the time and resources to think deeply about what it is they are doing and why they are doing it. Confronted with the often alien world of the Internet, many executives are tempted either to dismiss it as a fad or to adopt a wait-and-see attitude. These companies do so at their own peril. The only way to begin to understand the Net as it affects individual business practices and the economy as a whole is to embrace it, think about it, read about it, talk about it. In short, do that vision thing.

From the Suite of the CEO: A 12-Step Net Strategy Scenario

1. What's all this talk about the Internet?
2. Our main competitor is launching a Web site?
3. Maybe they know something we don't know.
4. Why didn't our team launch a Web site first? (The CEO doesn't know they wanted to.)
5. Let's hire a person in new media to work on this stuff.
6. Great site, folks. I especially like that corporate message from me you put in there.
7. Hey, let me show you my picture on this Internet!
8. What's this network budget item for next year?
9. It cost us how much?
10. Our projected return is what?
11. When?
12. Hey, whose idea was this Internet stuff?

If this sounds familiar to company executives, they're not alone.[1] A survey that included responses from 660 CEOs and other top executives in 11 information technology sectors demonstrates the confusion that many companies feel when using the Internet. While 70 percent of the respondents said it was important to have a company Web site, only a third actually did. Of those that had sites, 26 percent cited "product information" and 22 percent cited "image" as a reason. More interactive options, such as product sales and customer support, were reported in single or low double numbers. This survey suggests that these companies do not really understand the concept of interactivity, which is the linchpin of the Net's potential. And if IT company executives are having this trouble, imagine the confusion facing other business sectors!

On the surface, the Net appears to be just another medium of communication like print, television, cable, and radio. In the rush to establish their presence in this new medium, many companies have taken the information highway metaphor too literally. Home pages pop up overnight welcoming any and all to stop by for a visit. The only problem is that there isn't much behind these cyber billboards. On the Interstate, when you see a McDonald's sign that says, "6.2 miles to the left," you can be assured that the Big Mac you've been craving is ready and waiting for you 6.2 miles down the road and to the left. The billboard, in this case, is a way to direct traffic to a location. Home pages on the Net, however, are both billboards and front doors to businesses. Far too often, these front doors open either into nothing or into poorly repurposed brochures. They lack company vision.

VISION WITH PERSPECTIVE

The Internet isn't just another medium for communications. It is the circulatory system of the new, digital economy. A historical example illustrates the extent to which the Net can change the rules of business. Prior to Henry Ford's remarkable insight that mass production created a simultaneous need for mass consumers, Western economies generally adhered to a simple formula of "supply determines demand." Ford, with his $500 Lizzy and his 40-hour work week, reversed the formula. Mass production technologies pretty much guaranteed supply. Ford's genius was to recognize the need to create demand, or a mass market. In effect, the creation of a mass market broke the direct link between supply (material goods) and demand (consumers' pocketbooks). Value no longer rested in the tangible costs of production, but in the far less tangible concept of image or brand. Once value was placed outside the means of production, the economy was wide open to intermediary business practices and products. The rise of the mass market itself gave rise to entire industries designed to promote, package, and distribute products. Companies now take these practices for granted, an assumption that is one of the reasons it is so difficult for established companies to grasp the radical shift created by the digital economy. The whole approach to strategy is changing. An understanding of the Net business dynamics and having an endgame vision are essential to succeed in the Digital Estate.

Disintermediation is a good example of how radical shifts in the economy are manifest in business practices. Disintermediation is the process that eliminates the need for the middleman. Because the Net allows for direct communication between supplier and consumer, a third party to host or broker the transaction is superfluous. In this sense, the Net becomes the ultimate disintermediator. The real estate agent is disintermediated when buyers and sellers reach each other directly. The travel agent is disintermediated when travelers select from a number of destinations, analyze and compare rates, and directly book the best deal. Publishers and media companies are disintermediated when news and information are provided, say, by Reuters, directly to consumers, in real time. Think of it: The need for a middleman created by Ford's revolution is rendered obsolete by the evolution of the digital economy! For well established corporations designed to compete in a marketplace full of intermediaries, disintermediation creates confusion. (This transformation also creates new opportunities for new agenting, such as new ways of targeting using smart agents, which are dealt with in a later chapter.)

Leaders of the Digital Estate echo a resounding theme: Large, established companies are having a tough time with the dynamics of the Net. Many of those same people view the larger established companies simultaneously with delight and fear. From the Alley to the Valley, members of the Digital Estate repeatedly employ phrases like:

- "They just don't get it."
- "I dread the day when, and if, they get it."
- "They'll never get it."
- "Some of them are starting to get it."

The "it" they refer to is the magnitude of this move to a digital, internetworked world and what companies should do about it. The good news is that, once people and companies get it, they don't go back.

Established companies have the most to lose and, in many cases, the most to gain, in the digital environment. The Alley and the Valley companies know that the large companies can't move that quickly, but, if they do, it could prove disastrous for the smaller companies. It's like the parable of the tour guide in the Florida everglades, who points to hundreds of tiny fish trapped in swallows as the water dries. When the guide swirls the water with his hand, the fish scatter, flailing and flapping wildly. "The water's low," he explains. "They know they're just waiting to be eaten by the bigger fish, when they come."

Perhaps the biggest advantage for members of the Digital Estate is their shared sense of perspective. From the Alley to the Valley, these players recognize the Net as a business opportunity of astronomical proportions and set their sights accordingly. For them, the Net isn't just about advertising product, but about selling it! The Net is about finding consumers and connecting with them and about building ground-up businesses.

CLEARLY DEFINING THE ENDGAME

Unfortunately, established companies looking for business opportunity on the Net will find no single solution. Some, however, are successfully playing on this new field and setting the rules as they go. Despite the "on-the-fly" nature of the game, one of the single most important lessons for working in the Digital Estate is to clearly define the endgame. Companies need to know why they are doing what they are doing. They must "think themselves" down the road to *what* they want to be and *where* they want to end up. Then they have to devise a game plan to get there.

Engagement may be risky, but denial and wait-and-see strategies might ultimately prove fatal. Every day that an established company delays devising and deploying its Internet strategy, a hungry startup sets up shop determined to steal away the home court advantage offered by well-established brands, lucrative financing, and structural resources. As Halsey Minor, the 31-year-old CEO and Founder of CNET, notes: "If you're an incumbent, you have an advantage, but you're probably not smart enough to recognize it."[2] He clearly recognizes the value of brands, and is racing at breakneck speed to establish CNET as an electronic-household word. And he wants to do it before established companies, with stronger brand recognition than CNET, attempt to take his turf. "We know the successful brands do better in clutter, so branding for us is key."

THE CNET EXPERIENCE

Would-be competitors look at CNET, which stands for The Computer Network, as simply a location for people who care about technology. Minor, who sees his company as something quite different, doesn't mind. In fact, he's happy to have his competitors put him in the wrong pigeonhole. From the beginning—the company was founded back in 1992 as a cable TV programming service targeting people interested in computers and digital technologies—Minor wanted to impress the people, not the technology. To use one of his favorite expressions, success is measured in eyeballs, or, more precisely, in the number of eyeballs looking at CNET at any given time.

Minor originally pitched the idea for CNET to Microsoft cofounder Paul Allen, who has invested in excess of $1 billion in technology companies, and received more than $10 million in startup capital. When more than a million people a week were watching the television show, Minor viewed this as the tip of the iceberg. The San Francisco company outgrew its space in just months. It then took over a large health club next door, put in more studios, hired a fast-charging news team, plastered its "CNET" logo all over New York buses and Las Vegas taxi cabs, and went to work. Minor combined television with Web programming to build a multimedia company. The revenue ended up coming from the Internet part of CNET, from advertising dollars. So many visitors came to the site that it became very appealing to advertisers trying to reach those consumers. In fact, when WebTrack Information Services put out its first ranking of advertising revenue on the Web, CNET ranked in the Top 10.

CNET also deployed sophisticated technology that allowed it to target specific advertisements to specific people, and advertisers were willing to pay a premium to reach exactly who they wanted. Says Minor:

We follow the cable television model. One part of our service is advertiser driven. It's free to consumers. The second part is transaction-based. The third part is a-la-carte. Just like you have basic cable, pay or premium channels, and pay-per-view. Every part of our service, and everything we do, is designed to gain traffic. Remember, we're all about eyeballs. That's it.

In an effort to achieve that goal, CNET expanded its content. Not surprisingly, Minor is going all-out, never taking his own eye off the ball. Minor views the Net as a compilation of vertical niches and accordingly is targeting as many of those niches as fast as the company can launch products in each. Where CNET plays, it plans to lead. "In our news segment, we have a simple principle. We will report virtually every single news story that has to do with technology first. There will not be a story in a trade computer newspaper that you didn't see first on CNET." To achieve that objective, Minor raided leading technology publishers for top reporters who know the industry and had a knack for competition. Minor's success in becoming a major player in the Digital Estate rests in large part with his ability to clearly state the objectives for each tier of his enterprise and to passionately drive his staff to ride the laser.

To prove the point, the day that Microsoft agreed to include competitor Sun's Java product in Microsoft's operating system, a big story in the technology arena, *The Wall Street Journal* carried the story, giving credit to CNET for first reporting it. As a footnote, on that same day in the same newspaper, it was reported that *Encyclopedia Britannica,* the oldest continuously published encyclopedia in the world, citing fundamental changes in North American buying patterns, disbanded its sales force and officially ended its in-home encyclopedia sales in the United States and Canada. The operation had moved to the Net.

Oracle Goes Direct

It's not just the new companies that pick their target on the Net and shoot for the bullseye. Laurent Pacalin, Senior Director, Worldwide Web Revenue Strategies of Oracle, understood quite well the business potential in the growth of the Internet and figured out how to match it with Oracle's business objectives.[3]

Our challenge was to try to figure out how to penetrate the Wintel environment, which is the combination of Windows running on millions of personal computers and servers powered by Intel chips. Our traditional product, Oracle 7, was based on the Unix computer operating system. Selling Unix systems had been traditionally done on a one-to-one salesperson relationship. The PC environment is a one salesperson to many customers relationship. In mid-1994, we were looking for discontinuity in the distribution channel and the Net provided it.

Our business objective was to distribute our software product as broadly and as quickly as possible on a worldwide basis. We created an electronic sales environment on our Web site, and moved the process along the sales cycle, redefining ourselves in a space where we weren't. We offered a 90-day free trial of the product, because you need to create value. Some people thought they were going to lose their jobs, so we got global resistance from inside. Using the Net, we were the agents of change disrupting the sales staff's business practice. The concept was to move to electronic sales for the Wintel space.

The reality was that we were growing at such a rate that the sales force couldn't handle it in the traditional manner. The first thing we had to do was reconcile the current business environment. We positioned the Net as a sales assistant and educated internally. The definition of our product changed, from being in a box to being electronic. Using this method, the perception of the customer becomes more comprehensive. This can work for the insurance industry, for loans, or basically, for any product that can be made easy to find and easy to download or access on the Net. You have to rethink how you build your product.

In one year, we had 200,000 copies of the products downloaded. This is the try-and-buy mechanism. About half the people registered, and of those generally about eight to ten percent convert. We didn't have a "box-pusher" legacy reseller channel. We then created an online community. Look at the business dynamics. The costs of distribution were incurred by the customer, not the corporation. The cost savings have been huge, from packaging, mailing, and all that. We put the product on the server and people come and take it away. We were seeding the marketplace.

Don't try to take old stuff and tweak it to make it Web-ready. The way to go is jump in it. You can't figure where the Net is going, nobody knows. But in business, the rate of returns are getting shorter and shorter. Lifecycles are getting shorter. You need instantaneous rates of returns. Economics drive this, with the cost of goods and the costs of sales increasing. Using the Net, and defining exactly what we wanted to accomplish, helped us bring new customers quickly from awareness to purchase. Our online advertising wasn't for branding, it was value-based with a strong call for action, designed to start the sales cycle.

Netscape: The Legend Continues

The Netscape story has become the stuff of business legend, even when it was less than two years old. It goes something like this:

At 22, Marc Andreessen was an undergraduate at the University of Illinois, where he worked writing computer code for the National Center for Supercomputing Applications. Andreessen and fellow student Eric Bina began tinkering with the idea of designing a graphical interface for the World Wide Web, then an infant technology for linking the resources of the Internet that had been developed by Tim Berners-Lee at CERN, the European Laboratory for Particle Physics. During the winter of 1993, Andreessen and Bina wrote the basic codes for a browser and called it Mosaic. It became an overnight sensation. By the fall of 1994, Mosaic users accounted for 60 percent of all the traffic on the Web.

Andreessen shortly left the Midwest for Silicon Valley, where he met Jim Clark, a former Stanford University professor and founder of Silicon Graphics. Joining forces, the duo set out to conquer the Web. The first order of business was to displace the working prototype by building a better mousetrap, as it were. With $4 million from Clark, another $4 million from venture capitalists Kleiner Perkins Caufield & Byers, and a bunch of Andreessen's pals from Illinois, the team took only six months to release a beta version of what would eventually become the Netscape Navigator. On December 15, 1994, Netscape shipped its first commercial version. Within only four months, about 6 million copies of the Navigator were in use.

The point of this story, however, is not just that Andreessen is a brilliant designer or far-reaching visionary. In business terms, the real story is the strategy behind Netscape's unprecedented success. By concentrating on its endgame, to become the de facto standard browser for the Internet, Netscape was forced to invent new strategies to achieve that goal. First, the founders realized that the only way to compete with free copies of Mosaic was to offer free copies of the Navigator. Next, they used the Net as their very own worldwide distribution center, simultaneously creating demand and supply for their product. Still more importantly, Netscape did all of this by sidestepping traditional distribution channels. With no packaging, no retailers, no advertising, and no distribution costs, Netscape captured a full 75 percent of the Internet browser market.

FOCUSING THE VISION

CNET, Oracle, and Netscape tell the same basic story. They all focused clearly on their end goals. The following examples address more specific problems encountered in the move to the Net and the strategies of some companies to overcome them.

WHY ARE WE DOING THIS?

Businesses are in business to make money, presumably while achieving other company goals. A case in point is the story behind USA Today Online. The newspaper *USA Today* gained its current position by following a clearsighted strategy to become the first cityless, daily newspaper in the United States. When it came time to tackle the Net, *USA Today*, like many big companies, leaped into cyberspace towing its historical business concepts. It first launched a paid product on the commercial online service CompuServe. Not a lot of people paid; so it backed off. Then *USA Today* released software for people to access its Web site, charging $12.95 per month for three hours access to its online newspaper, $2.50 for every hour beyond that. After four months, the site had signed up only about 1,000 subscribers. The company ultimately began phasing out the software and opened its Web site to the Net for free. USA's learn-as-you-go strategy paid off.

Here's what they found:

1. They didn't need to be in the Internet access business.
2. You can't compete with "free" by charging admission.
3. You have to be willing to roll with the punches, admit mistakes quickly, learn from them, and rethink on the fly.

USA Today initially treated the Web as an outlet, a sort of cyber-newsstand. Their motive in using the Web was to cash in on stray subscribers rather than to distribute the news.

One of the biggest mistakes a company can make in going on the Web is not knowing why they are doing it. Even if the only reason a company is on the Web is because they see others doing it, they should admit it. Then they should look at their early presence as an opportunity for learning and staying in-tune with the Web environment. Good research generally precedes successful development, especially genuine, real-time, on-the-fly research!

WE'RE NOT BROKEN, SO WHY DO WE NEED FIXING?

It seems that Bill Block, the head of the New Media Division at supertalent agency ICM (International Creative Management), and other agencies were having trouble understanding just how the Internet would affect their business. After all, they contract stars out to big budget moviemakers, and no one believes that Hollywood and the Silver Screen are going to be undermined by the Net. "It's not clear where the rubber meets the road on all this," says Block.[4] Similarly, Lewis Henderson of the William Morris Agency says, "You have to play today in order to play tomorrow."[5] It is sometimes hard, however, to play when you don't understand the game.

Talent agencies are a good example both of the challenge confronting intermediary businesses, and of the need to define your endgame. The major studios initially focused on using the Net primarily as a new promotional outlet for the latest films. Most studios have interactive departments. Agencies are also setting up interactive divisions, but agencies are in the habit of thinking of talent as working for someone else. However, many interactive artists—musicians, actors, writers, designers, composers, etc—are not necessarily interested in working exclusively for the studios. They also are interested in pursuing their own projects, which need financial backing. These artists need a different kind of representation. If agencies define their endgame as providing talent to the studios, they might limit an opportunity to broaden the base of their business.

ISN'T THIS JUST ANOTHER TECHNO-TREND?

Listen to the far-reaching goals of some of the most aggressive players on the Net, and one thing becomes crystal clear: The Internet is not about technology, but rather about opportunity. Never let technology stand in the way of your mission. Listen to such companies as The Internet Fashion Mall, whose advertising boasts, "We have but one goal—to change the way the fashion industry does business," or to Compucard (CUC), whose stated mission is "to become the nation's leader in content across all areas of consumer spending." Companies like these are banking on the long-term consequences of doing business over the Internet and accommodating the short-term limitations of current technology.

Another Digital Estate company illustrates the need to separate the technological bells and whistles from the endgame strategy. Starwave, whose ESPNET SportsZone is one of the most popular sites on the Web, has a goal of building a networked interactive multimedia business that can compete with any consumer publisher, regardless of the medium. According to David Ticoll of the Alliance for Converging Technologies, Starwave belongs in anyone's top five list of networked interactive media consumer publishers most likely to succeed.[6] After spending the first year concentrating on building their technology base—online, CD-ROM, interactive TV—Starwave shifted to a consumer focus: What do sports fans really want to know? For Starwave, the company mission is to become the clearinghouse for sports by giving sports fans, i.e., consumers, what they want and when, where, and how they want it. Starwave avoids the technology trap by grasping the true significance of the interactive consumer. The trap is to confuse the technology and techno-talk surrounding the Internet with the needs of the consumer. The Internet is a means to an end and not an end unto itself. The difference is in recognizing that the telephone became an essential appliance because it facilitated conversation, not because it was novel technology.

Obsession for the Digital Estate

Clear definition of an endgame, the digital mission statement, or a focused vision tops the list of attributes of leaders in the Digital Estate. When Microsoft chief Bill Gates ultimately saw the monumental proportion of the potential power of the Net, he refocused the entire company to be Internet-centric, incorporating Internet technology into all Microsoft products, repositioning the company to be a Digital Estate company.

As the market expands in countless directions, and as millions of businesses and consumers become networked together, these leaders keep their eyes on the ball and drive their companies to follow.

When asked to define their Net strategies, the leaders, without hesitation, utter a clear, focused statement that is articulated within seconds. They actually *live* that Vision Thing.

THE BATTLE OF THE BRANDS

Some in the Digital Estate say that the old brands have no place in the new world, that they either will need major makeovers or should stay off the Net, doing what they know best. Just as established organizations and new companies grapple with new business models in the Net environment, organizing communities of interest and defining their ultimate business objectives, so too are there conflicts when it comes to creating, maintaining, or extending brands. Will legacy brands be an asset or a deficit in an internetworked world? How do established companies play in the new arena: by brand extension or by creating totally new brands? How do newcomers gain recognition and increase market perception?

When World Wide Web usage first exploded in 1995, the question was which aspects of the value chain would be most strategic to exploit? Between the provider of information and the user of information, there was a lot of play. Most well-known companies approached the Net as a place to transfer what they did into a knowledge base for consumers: Fidelity promoted its investment portfolio, MCI promoted its long-distance service, and IBM promoted its technology. Meanwhile, the companies that advertised in traditional media simply transferred what they did into the new media. As the environment matured, companies realized that they too could provide content and services directly to consumers, and many changed or adapted their approach to the changing medium. Even Madison Avenue took note, with companies like Nabisco creating the Nabisco Cyberhood, complete with health tips, calorie

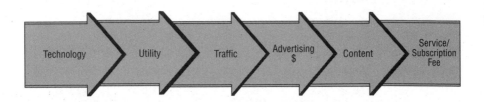

FIGURE 9-1

counters, and the latest promotions from its leading brands, including Oreo, Grey Poupon, and Barnum's Animal Crackers.

A BRAND BY ANY OTHER NAME ...

As the number of women and children using the Net skyrockets, driving toward a mass market, companies will face new opportunities and challenges in branding in the new medium. Web sites including detailed company information will be considered the baseline entry point for participation, as consumers push companies away from static billboard messages to interactive, information-rich streams. Companies will be pressed to build and strengthen relationships with their customers, who will be quick to provide feedback, and goods and services will be purchased from new as well as from trusted brands. In the Digital Estate, companies filter into four categories, each of which has its merits:

- New brands by old brands
- New brands by new brands
- New and unexpected products by old brands
- Old brands in new territory

NEW BRANDS BY OLD BRANDS

The Net provides great opportunity for established companies to create new brands, which may be broader and stronger than in the traditional business environment. New brands have certain advantages, not the least of which may be less friction within the home office. They offer a way for companies to compete with themselves without appearing that way, at least to the team keeping the established business running. As companies enter the Net space as a new medium, they encounter new modes of operation. Errors and missteps are expected. Introducing a new brand entails less risk of damaging the core brand and offers more opportunity to grow freely within the new medium. This approach has been successfully executed by several companies, notably several major media companies who had the choice, since they were among the first to introduce large-scale, content-based sites.

- When Conde Nast Publications, publishers of *Vogue, Glamour, Details, GQ,* and *Mademoiselle,* entered its brands on the Net, it started with both Conde Nast Traveler, named directly after its print publication, and Epicurious, a new brand. After newcomer Epicurious received four times as many visits as Conde Nast Traveler, the company moved Traveler under the Epicurious umbrella. Its next electronic product line was called Swoon, a content area focusing on romance, sex, and relationships for 18- to 34-year-olds. A majority of the content was original, with a small portion from the company's magazines.

- When Hearst Magazines launched on the Net, it opted to create a new product, called *Home Arts,* which culled information from the Hearst publications. It created new content packages by pulling select content from the print publications.

- The *Boston Globe,* owned by The New York Times Company, entered cyberspace under the umbrella of Boston.Com, creating a new brand for a new medium, at the same time aggregating other news and information providers in the New England area.

- Time Inc. housed its well-known publications, including *Time, People,* and *Sports Illustrated,* on its umbrella site called Pathfinder. It became one of the most-visited content sites on the Web. Says Bruce Judson, General Manager of Time Inc. New Media, "Because of the unique nature of the Internet, we could develop a new brand with lasting value, and reinforce the value of our individual properties."[1]

NEW BRANDS BY NEW BRANDS

Just as the Internet will cause a massive restructuring of the computer industry, it will also effect a restructuring of brands, as new companies emerge and thrive, because they will provide true service and valuable products. Leading companies in the Digital Estate quickly identify emerging needs, then pounce on concepts to fulfill those needs. Established companies will be faced with either leading, fast following, or watching from the sidelines. This trend opens the way for new power brokers, those who seek to aggregate other brands under "superumbrellas." When CNET decided to enter the navigation arena, rather than launch its own branded search agent, it simply created a new brand called search.com and aggregated all the major search agents under that umbrella.

Since the landscape essentially is flat on the Net, one of the strategies successfully deployed by leaders of the Digital Estate is to stake out ground, capture the hill, and create the impression that they are the dominant new player in a particular arena. This strategy has continually paid off, as the better-known, established companies play with only one foot in the interactive waters. The new competitors deliver true utility to consumers in the digital environment, while many established companies simply attempt to deliver advertising and marketing messages online.

- SportsLine USA is an online service devoted exclusively to sports information, entertainment, and merchandise. The Florida company launched its service after identifying that the online industry was an explosive market, based on subscribers and potential revenue. The company received financial backing from several well-known companies, including New York Life, Kleiner Perkins Caufield & Byers, Reuters, and TCI. It offered up-to-the-minute scores, contests, real-time chats with sports figures, as well as sports shopping.

- The Internet Shopping Network, a division of the billion-dollar television retailer Home Shopping Network Inc., became one of the largest online computer retailers, with more than 25,000 computer hardware and software products for sale. The company advertised heavily throughout the Web to build its name recognition and drive traffic to its site.

- Hot Wired, the well-known Web site, was launched shortly after *Wired Magazine*. Rather than repurposing content from its print sibling, Hot Wired created its own original content and communities, and then branched out further by launching a search engine called HotBot and a book publishing arm called Hardwired.

The lightning speed at which a brand can get established on the Net is alarming to some established companies. When Internet directory operator Yahoo! started, usage and growth occurred by word of mouth. The founders say they chose the name Yahoo! because they consider themselves yahoos. But the name was earlier purported to stand for "Yet Another Hierarchical Officious Oracle." Whatever its true origins, the name evoked chuckles in the marketplace. How could a serious search tool be called Yahoo!? After all, database tools from the traditional computer industry carried such serious and heavy-duty names as dBase and Informix. The chief Yahoos kept enhancing their listings, and the company eventually went public in one of the most successful initial public offerings in history, raising $37 million and making the chief Yahoos multimillionaires. The company poured the money back into advertising, including spots on the Late Show with David Letterman. The campaign, aimed at people curious about the Internet, was themed, "Do You Yahoo?" Yahoo! became an Internet-household word. The company then extended its brand into print, by partnering with publisher Ziff-Davis to create the magazine *Yahoo! Internet Life*. Then it went on to launch local editions dubbed Yahoo! San Francisco, Yahoo! New York, Yahoo! Los Angeles, Yahoo! Japan and Yahoo! Canada. It also created My Yahoo!, a customized version for personalized content. The company started as a technology provider and evolved to content provider (Fig. 9-1).

NEW AND UNEXPECTED PRODUCTS BY OLD BRANDS
(CURVE BALLS)

In the Digital Estate, brands can be leveraged to extend products into new arenas, a trend that stretches from Silicon Valley (and Redmond) to Madison Avenue. When Microsoft decided it wanted to be a global news provider, it created MSN News, which started first on Microsoft's proprietary network, but ultimately moved to the World Wide Web. To extend even further, Microsoft partnered with NBC to create Internet-based products on a number of topics, including news, finance, sports, and entertainment, in an effort to become a global news provider. Critics took note when noted broadcast journalists Michael Kinsley and Linda Ellerbee joined the venture to create online news programs. This put Microsoft on a collision course with traditional news organizations, such as *The Wall Street Journal*, Time Warner, and *The New York Times*. The Net provides an unprecedented opportunity for companies to establish themselves in new areas and to extend their past brands.

AT&T also decided to be a supplier of general information to consumers by launching a service that aggregated news stories from major publications each day. Called LeadStory, the service picked a major topic each day and linked throughout the Web to consolidate information. AT&T also targeted businesses with information, such as directories, demographic information, and marketing advice.

Even Madison Avenue is moving in the direction of providing content areas of interest, primarily so that consumers and providers might spend more "quality time" together. One such effort was from toothpaste company Colgate-Palmolive. In addition to clearly stated product information, the company provided a Grand Canyon tour, targeted to families, replete with personal trip reports from previous travelers, maps, grand photos, and itineraries for families and children.

It's not difficult to envision a next step. A company might offer travel packages to specific family vacation spots, including full-service reservations and ticketing; it might provide real-time discussion groups of travelers or those interested in a particular trip. A commodity (toothpaste) supplier thus transforms itself into a community organizer, a valuable service provider, and a trusted advisor! And it probably wouldn't hurt toothpaste sales.

OLD BRANDS IN NEW TERRITORY

Nowhere have attempts to extend and leverage brands into electronic media been more aggressive than in the sports arena. When the National Hockey League partners with IBM for the all-star Web site, the National Football League partners with Microsoft for the Superbowl, and *Sports Illustrated* promotes its swimsuit issue on the Pathfinder site, it becomes clear that the major brands are not planning to leave the digital environment to newcomers. Brand extension efforts on the Net sometimes start out as promotions, but they evolve into new products or services.

One example is when the NHL partnered with IBM to extend the league's brand, using data collection and storage technology at every game throughout the league to create new, interactive products and services, leveraging each team's brand, to create merchandising that could be sold with it on the Net.

With the perfect sports demographics, athletic equipment manufacturers, credit card companies, and airlines were an easy early sell. Schick Shaving Products Group even decided to underwrite the "Rookie Report," which featured content about NBA rookies, as well as the Schick Rookie Game, an all-star weekend event. Here are some additional examples:

- To extend its presence, the National Football League collaborated with The Weather Channel, to provide users with game-day weather forecasts and links to the NFL. The Weather Channel online did the same for ski conditions at more than 200 resorts around the world.

- 1-800-Flowers was one of the more successful businesses on the Net. In addition to its interactive store, which encouraged users to log on and send the perfect gift for any occasion, the company extended its services to include information about growing and arranging flowers. The move might have been obvious, but it *was* successful as a brand extension.

In addition to creating totally new products for an internet-worked world, companies also have an opportunity to transfer some of their current products.

Since it was founded in 1971, Lexis-Nexis has been delivering content online. Originally designed as a business news and research service for lawyers who could connect to mainframes through dumb terminals to conduct legal research, the company's databases are extensive. They include Supreme Court decisions as they are handed down, state codes, U.S. codes, case books, international laws, law review articles, journals, and almost all primary research materials found in a law library. The service proved to be invaluable, and Lexis-Nexis became a term as familiar in legal circles as a tort.

The company realized early that the best way to brand its service as an essential tool for the legal industry was to provide it free to law schools. Each year thousands of graduates grew dependent on it. The strategy worked, and law offices now consider Lexis-Nexis charges a general operating expense. Firms that can't afford the service can always access the data through their state, county, or city library Lexis-Nexis terminals.

The problem that faced the company, owned by Anglo-Dutch publishing giant Reed Elsevier, was how to extend its brand, which included a massive database of more general business and professional information as well as the legal databases. The company's goal was to make Lexis-Nexis available to every major desktop platform, via every major e-mail system, and through the Internet. The company adopted a more flexible pricing structure. It now includes an annotated Web service that lets users browse headlines and synopses of documents, which can then be downloaded for a fee.

HOW TO CREATE GREAT BRANDS ON THE NET

CREATE GREAT PRODUCT

- ESPNET and Starwave created SportsZone, a totally comprehensive sports location, featuring all the latest scores and statistics, down to the regional level. It carries more than 20,000 electronic pages of information.

- Ragu's community of "Mama's Cucina" is an entertaining, food-filled environment with recipes and attitude that mirror that of the audience.

- Digital Equipment Corp. created AltaVista, arguably the fastest search mechanism on the World Wide Web. The search engine was so good that by word of mouth alone it received 300,000 hits on the first day of launch, 600,000 on the third day, and 1.5 million on its fifth day. It soon became one of the most-used search services on the Web. Originally, the company expected to extend the Digital Equipment Corp. name, but after users came to know the product as AltaVista, Digital decided to create a line of AltaVista products, ranging from firewalls to security programs and e-mail. Though the search engine was free, like most others on the Web, the company recognized the opportunity to quickly establish market share in an exploding market and to worry about the revenue model later.

CREATE USEFUL SERVICE

- Alamo, in addition to providing all its rental car locations, also serves up travel information, weather for destination cities, coupons, games for children, and chat areas.

- Mobil took a service-oriented approach, detailing the issues of the day and providing a direct e-mail service to congressional representatives, including customized addressing based on the user's zip code entry. As sponsors of Masterpiece Theatre, the company also includes a calendar of upcoming shows as well as online credit card applications.

- Goodyear furnishes safety information, including proper tire pressure and driving tips. When consumers include their year and make of car, a tire locator instantaneously makes a tire recommendation and supplies the location of their nearest dealer. Included is the schedule for an American icon, the Goodyear Blimp. It is not hard to imagine seeing the blimp as an advertisement on a Superbowl Sunday site, where a click of the blimp would provide a real-time aerial view of the game.

- Mars' M&M's site provides helpful baking tips, especially on how to make the best use of chocolate.
- Ford includes a personal financial planner that calculates how much disposable income a consumer might have after all other living expenses. The service includes a lease and a purchase calculator.

CREATE WHAT IS EXPECTED

- Walt Disney Co. not only created one of the ultimate entertainment locations on the Web, complete with its branded movie trailers, sound clips, and Disney theme park tours, but also created a family-oriented location including local listings of children's activities.
- Minolta created a location with thorough product literature on the company, including advance looks at new offerings.
- Cadillac listed details on all its product lines, by model, with photos and specifications.
- *The New York Times* created a daily metropolitan newspaper information package, with serious tone, smart graphics, and frequent updates.

CREATE WHAT IS NEEDED

- Lycos, the search engine company, created an in-depth directory of the World Wide Web, which grew as the complexity of the Web content grew.
- Pointcast created a product that permitted information to be sent from the Internet directly to consumers, so that they didn't have to spend additional time searching for information they regularly used. It appeared on users' computers as a screensaver with information and hot links.
- RealAudio created technology that allowed consumers to hear audio over the Net in real time.

The media industry, whose advertising revenue is at risk, has been particularly challenged by the issue of branding on the Net. One of the largest, The New York Times Company, owners of *The*

New York Times, The Boston Globe, several regional newspapers, and television stations, pursued a strategy of corporate investment in individual business units, including an off-site group that created the Internet versions of *The New York Times.* The overall effort has been overseen personally by Lance Primis, President and Chief Operating Officer of The New York Times Company, who is one of the more forward-thinking CEOs of the media industry.[2] His views:

> In order to be an effective provider of great information in the new electronic media, you'll have to have developed strong brands. Advertisers will then pick the distribution they trust and strong information brands will help distinguish the medium of choice. If branded advertisers don't keep the brand strong, they can be replaced. You need to keep investment up, promote it well, and provide digital outlets. Partnership will be key in this new electronic medium as content providers will have to partner with distributors. Our intent is to pursue a brand new kind of journalism in the electronic world. But for the next ten years, we see most of our revenue from what we own, in new forms. Until the capabilities of the Web expand—like motion and interactivity—it is unlikely that established companies and their advertising agencies will spend a great deal of their advertising budgets in the new medium. There will still exist the pressure of time management by the consumer. Many of our potential readers cite "no time" to read as the reason for not subscribing. It will be interesting to see how "no time" impacts Web usage even though consumers can sort their own material. Companies like ours need the proper tension between the traditional and the new. Then, ultimately, you'll see integration of the businesses. You'll see sort of a refinery where the information is collected once and then gets very targeted. We're counting on high quality, preemptive information generated by a superb staff. Also, we'll have a better chance of keeping our talent if we have more outlets. Great branded content doesn't have to be first. It can be second and win.

OPPORTUNITY FOR BRANDS WITH VALUE

Brands on the Net, whether new or old, can also aid in enhancing a company's image. A case in point is AltaVista, which has enhanced the reputation of Digital as a Net-savvy company with sophisticated technology. The creation of the new brand was an un-expected benefit. Similarly, new products from Wired enhanced that company's image as not only Net-savvy, but also highly astute in business and brand extension.

In a fast-paced, information-loaded, internetworked environ-ment, there will be a lot of clutter, as thousands of companies try to reach the ever-growing Internet population. Consumers will be attracted to the brands and services that provide the highest value, those that reward users, offer good prices, and are personalized. This environment will provide tremendous opportunity for the best known brands to stand out, whether those brands started in the past or are new in the Digital Estate.

TARGETING THE MASSES, ONE AT A TIME

There's been a lot of talk about mass customization, but the Net turns all that on its head. The formula for it is simple enough: Reach the right person, at the right time, in the right place, with just the right message. Driven by the desire to more accurately market products and services to select individuals, marketers foresaw the end of costly, wasted messages on either the wrong people or on people who should care but don't. The problem, of course, has been finding a medium suited for such a far-reaching goal.

The Net is that medium. Mass customization is inherent in the Digital Estate, with targeting perhaps the greatest added value of all the internetworking capabilities. The artificial intelligence and smart agent technologies that are transforming the Net into a marketplace have been under development in university labs for many years. The prospect of mass numbers of networked consumers, however, is ultimately pushing these technologies out of the labs and into the marketplace.

Marketing pioneers in the Digital Estate are discovering the extent to which a digital environment, enhanced by digital delivery systems, changes the relationship between the consumer and the marketing message. In this medium, advertising messages can be customized to fit the individual consumer with little effort or waste because the consumer comes after the message rather than the message tracking down the consumer. The challenge is to find ways to utilize these technologies as they grow and develop as an integral part of the Web.

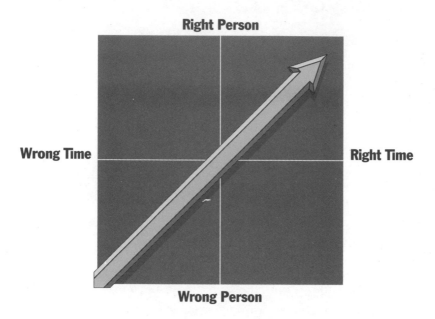

THE DIGITAL ESTATE

TARGETING DYNAMIC

Right Person

Wrong Time

Right Time

Wrong Person

FIGURE 10-1

TARGETING FROM THE INSIDE OUT

The two predominant ways that marketers reach consumers are direct mail and advertising. While each has its advantages, both fall far short of the ideal of one-on-one marketing. The basic strategy for either approach can be viewed as the *outside-in* model for reaching the consumer with advertising or information. Companies carpet-bomb consumers with messages, and eventually enough messages filter through to the right people.

In the Digital Estate, just the opposite happens. Specific messages and advertisements are provided to consumers at the precise moment that the information is desired. (See Fig. 10-1.) This is what I call the *inside-out* model. The first phase of this targeted approach was highlighted by the growth of community-based services, such as iVillage, CNET, and Match.com. Smart agents and targeting take the concept of community to its logical, final step: reaching the community of one at exactly the right moment.

By approaching the Net from the inside-out and by using resources such as smart agent technologies, marketers are learning how to confront four fundamental challenges in advertising:

- *Targeting/market segmentation:* Reaching only your target audience, with the ability to customize your message
- *Reach:* Getting to more members of your target audience
- *Frequency and duplication:* Eliminating under- or overexposure
- *Measurability:* Determining what worked in a timely manner

SNAIL MAIL LIBERATED

Direct mail starts with lists, some with millions of names, of people who buy certain products, who live in certain zip codes, who went to certain schools. There are credit card lists, credit history lists, high traveler lists, lists of people with children, and even lists of lists. Companies rent these lists from list brokers, and deliver their messages to the people whose names found their way onto the lists. The direct mail industry has gotten quite good at this over the years. Since third-party companies handle the mailings, the companies renting the lists don't take possession of the names, leaving the first company with ownership of the list.

On the recipient's end, whatever mail hits home the consumer deems as useful, targeted information, while that which is not relevant is junk mail. When a magazine is looking to attract new subscribers, it typically mails several million pieces of promotional material. Even though the company might give consumers the incentive by offering free calculators or a chance to win prizes, if only seven out of every hundred people respond positively, it is considered a home run. Even though there is plenty of waste, everyone knows the formula, and it has worked predictably for decades.

Some say that the Net is closest to the direct mail model, but that's not totally true. In the traditional direct mail model, the seller rents names and reaches out to blanket those consumers. In the

Digital Estate, consumers preselect themselves. It is not necessary to use intermediaries or brokers, and the concept of paying for waste is foreign. At the time of receiving the message, the consumer is more likely to be receptive, since Net messages can be targeted within relevant information, providing context for the consumer.

The Net can totally redefine direct marketing, potentially disintermediating the list brokers and the mail companies and having a dramatic impact on the direct marketers themselves. The Internet adds a new component to the projection formula. Advertising on the Net can become a service when correctly targeted, providing pertinent information based on consumer preferences. As previously mentioned, California coupon veteran Money Mailer put its entire database of millions of coupons on the Web for local, regional, and national consumer services and products. With the click of a button, users can print coupons for discounts at the local McDonald's and Burger King, or at local businesses, from car washes to manicurists. Because Money Mailer distributes paper coupons to more than 100 million U.S. households weekly, it can cross-promote the print and electronic coupons, with Internet addresses on the paper versions. In the digital version, the coupon becomes a shopping service, selected by consumers for use when it matters most to them. There is no waste.

The bottom line with direct mail is to have more successes with each attempt at the mailing. On the Net, messages go to those who need to find them, which translates into a higher success rate.

ADVERTISING WHEN IT IS NEEDED

In the traditional advertising world, payments are based on CPM, or cost per thousand of people reached by the message. Television traditionally has the lowest CPMs, because millions of people are reached, making the cost per commercial high. While all the viewers might not be exactly the right recipients for the message, millions of them tune in to see *60 Minutes* or *Roseanne*. Specific interest magazines traditionally have the highest CPMs, because they are going to people who are primarily interested in the subject matter. This explains why tennis magazines carry mostly tennis advertising, technology publications are filled with advertisements for computers, and fashion magazines are supported by clothing advertisements.

Although many marketers treat the Net as a broadcast medium, it is actually a communications medium. When paired with smart agent technology, it provides the most potent of marketing capability, enabling companies to fully utilize the medium, rather than treating it as an extension of existing business practices. Unlike television, where consumer behavior is tracked by representative studies and viewership of shows is projected by extrapolating patterns among Nielsen families, consumers on the Net can be reached one at a time, with detail down to the lowest level.

When Internet home pages started multiplying and consumer usage exploded, companies naturally transferred advertising messages to the Net. This came to be known as billboard or banner advertising, even though the ads were often small strips at the bottom of home pages, hardly the look the name connotes. Two dynamics that are changing the nature of Web ads are the advancements in targeting and tracking technologies and the rapid sophistication of marketers who understand how the Net enhances one-on-one marketing. Here are a couple of scenarios to demonstrate the potential:

> *Scenario 1:* You are Volvo and you want to sell more cars to 35-year-old males in Chicago. You purchase banner advertising on the following sites: The Chicago affiliate of city.net to enhance local reach; CNET, the computer network site, to reach 35-year-old males with high disposable income; and Yahoo!, the search engine company, for broad reach to millions of consumers. City.net inserts the Volvo advertising message only to consumers in Chicago who view specific information, such as certain restaurant reviews or real estate listings consistent with the local demographic of a 35-year-old male. CNET inserts the Volvo ad only on pages viewed by people from Chicago locations, specifically, those with the best corporate addresses. Yahoo! presents the Volvo ad only to people who search for anything related to cars, especially if they have searched for anything to do with Volvo's main competitors.

In this hypothetical case, the car company reaches exactly whom it wants, and the cost of advertising is dramatically lower than in television or print. Also the company finds out within days if it is successful, since city.net, CNET, and Yahoo! all provide instantaneous itemizations of which people in their respective markets were presented with the ad.

> *Scenario 2:* You are Ford and you want to provide more targeted messages to people as they move along the purchase cycle. You buy advertising space on the five sites that receive the most visitors. These sites all subscribe to a context-matching Internet company that combines three unique databases: advertising information, individual profile information, and a context-based tracking database. A user visits one of the sites and reads a story about cars. This is presumed to be a potential target. The next day, this person, now identified as being in the correct demographic, based on a personal profile and a geographic location, reads a couple of stories, one from the online version of *Car and Driver* and another from *Consumer Reports* (a definite target!). Smart agent technology identifies the context of what he is reading: A story about imported cars (not good news for Ford!). The advertising database, in real time, inserts an advertising message on the commercial page highlighting the advantages of American cars. The consumer clicks on that ad (a definite target buyer!). The consumer is driven to a specific part of Ford's online presence that provides the comparison of long-term costs, maintenance, and longevity of various brands. A different ad is pulled from the advertising database (an ad within an ad!) to offer the consumer a special incentive discount just for answering a few questions. The consumer bites and answers a short questionnaire, which gives the database more information to better target the consumer's needs. It turns out that convenience of service is critical. Since the consumer's path around the Net is tracked, it is determined that, based on what the consumer looked at, this person is also considering a Lexus. The next time the consumer visits one of the five sites where Ford is advertising, the Ford ad is a Ford-Lexus comparison, highlighting features that give Ford an advantage over Lexus. The next visit to one of these sites produces a very special, personalized message from Ford: "How would you like a free test drive this weekend? We'd be happy to have the car at your home anytime Saturday or Sunday. Click here to tell us the best time." The consumer clicks, fills in a time, and an e-mail message is automatically routed to the nearest dealer. The Ford dealer is then able to connect with potential

buyers, at the most convenient time, in the most convenient location, with the assurance that purchase motivation, comparison shopping, and concerns all have been preaddressed. What is that customer worth to the local dealer at that moment? Lots. Instead of paying for the advertising in rates, the dealer pays based on the quality of traffic and sales conversion rate.

Even though these hypothetical examples involve big ticket items, the scenario can be extended to Madison Avenue consumer products. Someone looking at fashion sites might be a target for the Fall line from Calvin Klein. Nike might send tennis shoe ads to U.S. Open fans and basketball shoe ads to someone who checks Lakers scores regularly and who fits a certain purchasing profile.

As the technological capability matures, product messages will continually evolve with the consumer through the entire purchase cycle. This will bring marketers face-to-face with new sets of choices and responsibilities, as they walk a finer line between providing total service and invasion of privacy. In the car scenario, does the manufacturer tell the dealer what kind of consumer is being handed over? Does the information trickle all the way down to the dealer? While these issues and others will no doubt arise, and be dealt with, for members of the Digital Estate that is no cause for delay as they eagerly rush in and fill the gaps created by the exponential expansion of the Internet.

SLICING AND DICING

The full-page advertisement in a trade magazine reads:

> Want to reach college kids in the Midwest between 6 and 10 P.M. the week before Spring Break? Want to reach New York investment bankers who work on Wall Street and are planning to travel? Want to reach UNIX users who work in Fortune 500 corporations and have them see your ad banner 6 times in one month, but not more than 6 times?[1]

The answer is supplied by DoubleClick, the company supplying the ad.[2] DoubleClick exists to buy media on the World Wide Web. Like many companies in the Digital Estate, DoubleClick defined its mission—to be a media sales company—but then moved with the medium itself when it identified an opportunity to become something much bigger, with an added goal of targeting the masses, one at a time.

The story of DoubleClick also highlights how companies in the Digital Estate benefit by becoming intimate with the medium itself. These companies can monitor and spot new market dynamics, such as mass customization and highly targeted reach facilitated by the Web, and they can then move quickly and decisively to capitalize on these new opportunities and new alliances.

The advertising agency Poppe Tyson, a pioneer in Internet advertising, launched a division called DoubleClick to exclusively sell advertising to be run on companies' Web sites. DoubleClick received notoriety when it landed the prestigious Netscape account, the most visited site on the World Wide Web. A few months later, another company, Internet Advertising Network (IAN), was formed to create a system for advertisers to highly target their prospects when they entered an affiliated Web site in the network.

Says DoubleClick CEO Kevin O'Connor:

> In November, Poppe Tyson announced its intention to create a network of Web sites linked by powerful technology. This was identical to our own concept. Dave Carlick, the General Manager of Poppe Tyson, and I had a phone conversation in late December and within 15 minutes concluded we needed to merge our companies. Our visions were identical and our skill sets were complementary. We saw that by merging the number one media sales group together with the number one media technology group, we would quickly take the leadership position, and eliminate each other as competitors. We also realized that neither company was really capable of pulling if off alone. Poppe Tyson could never have developed the technology necessary and IAN could never have built a media sales organization in a timely manner.

In the Digital Estate, companies understand the fundamental linkage of product and technology, and realize that the New Media, in fact, needs to include new technology. Within four weeks, Poppe Tyson's division and Internet Advertising Network were merged into DoubleClick, a new company still with the objective of selling media, but with a new approach to provide sophisticated targeting capabilities for marketers.

DoubleClick built a network within a network, by signing on such companies as Quicken Financial Network, GE Business Pro, Travelocity, SportsLine USA, I-Golf, The Globe, Doonesbury, Excite, and United Media. These companies then made a slight change to the pages on their sites where they would allow advertising banners to be inserted by DoubleClick. The sites kept their own advertising efforts and used DoubleClick as an advertising supplement (and a revenue supplement) program.

DoubleClick could then approach potential advertisers, using its technology to forecast the number of targeted advertising impressions available and the total cost for those companies. The companies could select the types of sites where they wanted their advertising messages to appear, and set an upper limit on the number of impressions to stay within their budgets.

DoubleClick offered multiple target choices:

- *By Service Provider.* Advertisers could select users they desired to reach by Internet Service Provider (ISP), such a America Online, Compuserve, Prodigy, Netcom, or Pipeline. This allowed service providers to target people using competing services, with the capability of making the customer's special, introductory offers to switch services.

- *By Geographic Location.* Selection by country, state, telephone area code, and even zip code was offered.

- *By User's Operating System.* DoubleClick's technology could identify whether people were using Windows 3.1, Windows 95, Windows NT, Unix, OS/2, or Macintosh. Since engineers, scientists, and students are more likely to use Unix, creative individuals were more likely to use Macs, and software developers more likely to use Microsoft NT, affinity targeting was allowed.

- *By User's Browser Type.* By identifying the type of browser from companies such as Netscape, America Online, and Microsoft, companies selling browser software could target competitors.

- *By High-Level Internet Domain Type.* When an organization requests a domain name in the United States, it typically receives a suffix that describes the organization type. They are:

  .com for commercial business

  .gov for governmental agencies

  .edu for educational institutions

  .org for organizations

  .net for network providers

  .mil for military installations.

  Commonly available, this type of selection can identify and sort by suffix.

- *By Organization Type.* The Standard Industrial Classification System (SIC Codes), used by the United States government to classify organizations, are the recognized standards. SIC codes include organizations, schools, and the government. DoubleClick created a higher level set of categories that included organizations from multiple SIC codes and organizations lacking an adequate SIC code, such as Internet-related companies.

- *By Organization Size or Revenue.* DoubleClick created a database of organizations' and companies' sizes and revenues.

- *By Personal Interest.* DoubleClick tracked member Web site activity, and allowed advertisers to target their advertising messages to users based on their interests. Personal interest categories included business, finance and economy, educational and instructional, entertainment, government, politics, and military, health and medicine, news, recreation and leisure, science and technology, social science, sports, and travel.

- *By Days and Hours of Use.* By allowing specific times for advertising messages to be displayed, companies trying to reach business users could have their advertisements inserted between 9 a.m. and 5 p.m. Monday through Friday in local time, or only during hours when they were able to receive calls from target customers.

- *By Time Range.* DoubleClick allowed advertisers either to pace their advertising messages throughout a predetermined time frame, providing an evenly paced flow each day, or to blitz the target audience with messages until the desired number of impressions is achieved.

- *By Path.* DoubleClick tracks users when they click on an advertisement. It provides advertisers with information about which type of user seeks further information, providing the targeting company with data to modify their messages. Advertising messages can be changed on the same day.

DoubleClick symbolizes the targeting capabilities emerging in the Digital Estate. It offers a hybrid of direct response, through precise, measurable, and statistically projectable results, with advertising that features broad reach, low cost, and increased awareness. Because of DoubleClick's targeting capabilities, companies using the service receive results almost instantly, enabling them to test market products to specific consumer groups overnight and ramp their business accordingly. They get precise results more quickly and less expensively than they would through direct mail or traditional advertising.

"I'LL HAVE MY AGENT CONTACT YOUR AGENT"

Welcome to the world of agents. They started as Smart Agents. Then they became Intelligent Agents. On the Net, they can more accurately be defined as Intelligent Search Agents, since they are designed to sort through a mass of information in a somewhat intelligent manner. A sampling of agents demonstrates their value in targeting consumers on the Net.

- *Musical Selects.* Ex-MIT Media Lab spin-off, Agents Inc. makes recommendations about music, movies, and books by comparing one user's interest to the interests of other users with similar demographics. The technology is also targeted for various other interests, from books to helping people select Web sites that should interest them, based on comparisons with other users like them.

- *Shopping.* The Entertainment Connections shopping service targets demographically-focused advertisements and different sales pitches to consumers based on location.
- *Online/Offline.* Rather than surfing the Web manually, agents from companies such as Freeloader go out and bring you just what you want and then tell you when it's there. Your PC always has the latest, preselected information from the Net.
- *Screen Saver News.* After you don't use your PC for a few minutes, up pops news, weather, and selected stocks provided by Pointcast.
- *New News.* If you have time only to check out the new information that has been added on the Web since your last visit, agents from MilkTruck can do that automatically for you while you sleep.

Smart agents can do a lot of work for a marketer, but not all of it. They are incredible tools, to be sure, but they still depend on the creative insight of a user to be effective. Even with the agents, marketers must confront the unpredictable nature of the Net. Unlike other media, the Net is unique in its ability to "morph" with the momentary whims and needs of its users. Someone might log on to check the weather and decide to drop in at a virtual pub in London. A quick homework assignment just as quickly changes into an impassioned debate—or a romantic chat. Since predicting these whims is impossible, marketers have to develop strategies for targeting their audiences at the right time and in the right place. There are five targeting methods in the Digital Estate:

1. *Community.* Companies can customize messages of interest to appeal to specific people in specific communities. These can be by interest, such as in the case of a parents' discussion group, or geographically, such as in the case of a metropolitan city's dominant local site, maybe from a local newspaper.
2. *Content.* Billboards or banner advertising can be placed on specific pages of information. Companies reach the right person because the information at the location appeals most to their target audience.

3. *Context.* Advertising appears only in areas that are relevant to the content of your product. The concept is that companies will reach certain people only when they are absorbing information about the "desired" subject matter, that is, desired by the company that desires to reach that individual.

4. *Demographic and Psychographic.* This type of information is either volunteered by users or gathered from registration information that they provided about themselves in order to receive free services or information.

5. *Personal Behavior.* On the Net, a tracking technology commonly called "cookies" is implanted in consumers' software. This technology gives companies a way to track their visits to the Web sites. When a person visits a company's site, a small tag is embedded, not unlike the strip of wisdom wrapped up in a fortune cookie.

    This trail of crumbs or nuggets of information alerts online merchants to certain characteristics of the user. Cookies track a consumer's online movements and store the information on the user's own computer. The consumer brings along the information of past behavior on each visit to the site. In effect, the consumer knowingly (or unknowingly) tells the online merchant just what happened during a previous visit. This information allows merchants to customize and tailor their response to the customer. Thus, the cookie technology that links the consumer and the merchant becomes an added-value service. When the visitor comes to view certain content, in the time between the decision and the presentation of the information to the consumer, the individual's past preferences are identified and it is determined that a certain advertising message is appropriate for that individual, all within a fraction of a section, on a global basis. This is the technology that "remembers" a user's identity and password so that it never is entered again after the first visit.

    Accipiter, a North Carolina company whose goal is to set the next standard in interactive marketing, is one of a number of companies attempting to take this tracking to the next level. Accipiter dynamically combines three databases of information: registration data supplied by the individual, the context of what that person is viewing, and palettes of advertising, to supply different messages to different people based on who they are, where they're from, and their interests based on what they are viewing. Next comes the capability to track users' activities from site to site.

GETTING THE MESSAGE TO THE PEOPLE

By learning to see the Net from the inside out and by keeping an eye out for new means to target their messages, Digital Estate companies are inventing numerous ways to capture audiences and deliver specific messages. Here are a few examples:

- Interactive Imaginations created sophisticated games on the Net as a way to attract consumers who were ready to spend time competing for cash prizes. The catch is that the more demographic information a consumer gives, the more clues they receive to win. The consumers were challenged intellectually in the process. Advertisers receive guaranteed delivery of specific target audiences. Advertisers included Sprint, AT&T, Snapple, Capitol Records, and Toyota.

- Tracer created journey-oriented games, encouraging sleuthing for a fictional character in numerous Web sites. Advertisers' messages appear as part of the entertainment, much like product placements in movies.

- Jumbo Inc. created a site filled with 60,000 free shareware programs, in such categories as business, home and personal, games, and words and graphics. It inserted specific advertisements to target by domain, down to specific ads going to people from specific companies.

In each of these cases, the company is learning about the consumer without intermediaries. Companies will be able to track individuals not only by country, city, and zip code, but by neighborhood, purchase preferences, buying habits, Internet viewing profiles, and almost any other preference desired. Using laser-like consumer targeting, companies in the Digital Estate plan exactly who they want to reach, and when, with which message—one at a time.

THE RADICAL SHIFT
IN POWER

The Digital Estate gives new meaning to *customer empowerment.* On the Net, individuals can be the authors of their own worlds, both literally and metaphorically, and this assertion of authority has interesting implications, in both the home and the office. Leading companies in the Digital Estate have found ways to creatively tap into this sense of individualism, so that customers and employees achieve even more control, while the companies also benefit.

When on the Net, people are already interactive participants. While they are in this frame of mind, they might be willing to get their own information, create their own products, and search the enterprise databases themselves. The increase in user control increases their sense of responsibility and their desire to contribute. People go on the Net because it is interactive. So it makes sense that, while there, they will take every opportunity to interact. All they need are the tools.

Similarly, the internal extensions of the Internet, the corporate intranets, give employees a new way to participate in the mission of the company. Intranets remove many of the restrictions that have pushed companies toward bureaucratic organization. Centralized control of information is inefficient in a digital environment because it is unnecessary. Formerly, the *control* of information was power. In the Digital Estate, the *distribution* of information is power. In the network-centric world, the more a company gives away, or pushes out, to consumers or end users, the more widespread and powerful a company can become.

THE NEW THINKING ON EMPOWERING THE CUSTOMER

Encouraging interactive customer participation may seem daunting. The Net is big and there are many users. How can one company interact meaningfully with all these potential customers? Or, as commonly heard in Silicon Valley and Silicon Alley, "So many opportunities, so little time." Fortunately, the solution is relatively simple for companies willing to relinquish some control and re-think the dynamics of relationships among consumer, product, and producer. Getting customers to create products and do work is more than an option on the Net. It is considered a service and gives the term *customer authorization* a whole new meaning. The more the customer inputs, the more the company's costs decline, and the more the consumer feels empowered. What a concept!

There are various approaches to empowering the customers. Companies can get them to do the work or even get them to build the product.

1. PUTTING THE CUSTOMER TO WORK

In the Digital Estate, customers can easily tap into corporate databases on the Internet to access information, make purchases, or track the status of a service. Customer service is simply giving the customer access to the resources. This approach offers several advantages:

- The customer is free to access the information anytime, unhampered by work-week or work-day schedules.
- No one puts the customer on hold, so that there are no angry, frustrated tempers to soothe. Companies can use this opportunity to build affinity and assure great service.
- Letting the customer do the work also cuts company costs.

This strategy is already so successful and popular among end users that it is fast becoming a standard. All a company has to do is let go, liberate its information, and invite its customers in.

POWER TO THE PACKAGER!

It is not surprising that Federal Express took to the Net early and has commanded a significant presence there ever since. The Net is well-suited for the kinds of data-tracking that lay at the center of FedEx's business. Imagine moving more than 2.5 million items in 210 countries each working day, and keeping track of more than 500 aircraft, 37,000 vehicles, and nearly 300,000 Powership and FedEx Ship automated systems in an integrated global network. FedEx, however, sees itself as more than a transportation company moving cargo from point to point. It defines itself as a logistics link between customers and merchants.

Here's how FedEx manages its own logistics: A customer calls in with a pick-up. A service agent transmits the request to the company's tracking system, a database called COSMOS (customer, operations, management, and services). A message is sent to a regional dispatch center, which passes the pick-up information to a small computer located in each of the FedEx vans. The driver picks up the package, scans the attached smartbar code with a portable computer and keys in additional information, such as the destination zip code. Simply by returning the portable Supertracker to its port on the computer inside the van, the driver transmits information regarding the pick-up and destination to the regional dispatch center and from there back to the COSMOS database. After a package arrives at its destination city, it is scanned, sorted, and placed on a delivery van. Before taking off, the driver again scans the packages, and again transmits the data back to COSMOS through the regional dispatcher. Upon delivery, the driver keys in proof of delivery, which is transmitted to the database.

In moving to the Net, Federal Express opened this incredible database tracking system to individual customers. By entering an ID number, customers can determine the exact status of their package. Utilizing the Net in this manner was not a radical departure for FedEx, but rather an extension of their existing strategy to service their customers by empowering them. The Powership network automates shipping for clients by printing labels and calculating costs, as well as by providing a shipping and tracking service. By offering software integration, FedEx allowed its customers to function, in effect, as satellite sites. With nothing more than a PC and a modem, customers using the Powership network can request pickups, arrange billing, and track packages: no invoices, no hassle, no waiting, no delays. It's no surprise that about two-thirds of the company's transactions are currently handled using the Powership network.

UPS and Emery also launched Web tracking sites. The fit is natural, because it lets users do exactly what customer service representatives do. By using the Net, users save time and energy. Other industries are making use of the same idea with equal success.

- *Travel* is one of the more successful industries on the Web, because it is relatively easy to push the research and reservation function out to millions of wired consumers and businesses. While some airlines, such as Southwest and American, allow customers to directly check schedules, book flights, and choose seat assignments, other companies are using the Net to provide a new kind of travel service for their customers. Biztravel.com, for instance, aims to empower the frequent business traveler. Clients complete preference forms indicating everything from airline and seat preferences to athletic and dining preferences. Smart agents then prepare a portfolio. A businesswoman traveling to Chicago can book a flight and receive with the ticket a full packet of customized information about the area, including local news which may come in handy during her business meeting. The site also keeps track of frequent flyer mileage for the client. Other features of the site include an e-zine and bulletin boards for travelers to exchange tips. The user-generated content not only promotes community, but it enhances the service provided by the company by enabling customers to ask and receive exactly the information they need. Sabre has made its way to the Web with its site, Travelocity. Through the Net-based service, consumers can research and make reservations on almost any airline. In addition, the site has chat rooms, travel forums, a mall, content on travel events and schedules.
- *Real estate,* as an industry challenged by potential disintermediation, ironically has been trying to find ways to empower potential home buyers by allowing them to tap into their listing ser-

vices, showing that some are starting to get with the program. The National Association of Realtors instituted a Technology Conference and Exposition as part of its belief that survival depends on embracing high-tech tools and media. One of the key themes of the conference was finding ways to add value to the transaction by providing new services to Web sites. One service, Cyberhomes, provides real estate search capability with street-level interactive mapping. Another Net-based service called HomeScout helps home buyers search multiple databases on the Web from a centralized location.

- *Index Stock Photography* is one of many photography sites on the Web. Like text-heavy industries, photography, particularly the volume of photographs that make up the product of stock companies, is well suited for the Web. Customers can go to the site, search by keywords, download what interests them, think about it, play around a bit, and then order what they want. The customer does all the work.

2. HELPING THE CUSTOMER CREATE THE PRODUCT

While bringing customers into the production process is one way to utilize the interactive nature of the Net, giving them the means to create their own products is another. Personalized services that allow individuals to tailor information and access abound in the Digital Estate. Search engines have become as important an aspect of the ramp onto the World Wide Web as browsers. Online/offline delivery agents make tailored information a norm. However, another category for customization represents a new opportunity. Internet applications called *custom site generators* allow individuals to customize their own access to sites on the Web.

In their most basic form, home pages are the prototypes of this type of authoring tool. The site itself remains stable, with the content of the page remaining the same, while the information attached to the page becomes dynamic, through hot-links. Central control over content and links remains in the hands of the site's webmaster. Visitors can drop in and link out, but they cannot alter the site. Generators represent the next logical step, providing outside users with the tools to customize the site according to their own needs.

That's the concept behind CReAte Your Own Newspaper, better known as CRAYON. Designed by Jeff Boulton and Dave Maher while working toward an undergraduate degree in computer science at Bucknell University, CRAYON lets users create a customized newspaper by generating links to various media sources available on the Web.

It uses behind-the-scenes Unix scripts to custom-build a file of links to national, world, business, technical, entertainment, and other news sources, which the user draws from a menu. There are 95 options in 10 categories, including cartoons, such as Dilbert, horoscopes, quotes of the day, weather maps, and other items that regularly appear in printed newspapers every day. Should users wish to include a site not currently on the menu, they just type in the name and URL of the site. To further personalize the service, users can name their newspapers and even give them slogans. CRAYON then generates a page, which the user can save to hard drive. The value of the free service rests in linking individuals directly to host sites. Users get the news they want from the sources they choose when they want it.

Mass customization is one of the most radical opportunities created by the Net and a service that is growing in demand and popularity. In addition to CRAYON, InfoSeek, Individual Inc., and *The Wall Street Journal* are just a few sites that offer customization services. The reason for the demand is simple: The combination of the Net and the advancement of technologies like intelligent agents and customization software has shifted the balance between what consumers want and what they can have. Because consumers can customize with little effort or expense, they want to customize.

The final step in the equation, which will continue to emerge as the numbers on the Net reach critical mass, is the perception that customization is a right of the environment. This notion directly confronts years of thinking in terms of mass production as prerequisite for mass distribution, and it is a cause of apprehension for some companies. In the Digital Estate, where distributive thinking is the norm, the prospects of mass customization make perfect sense. It is a matter of finding business models that mirror or mimic the nature of the Net.

As a vast system of distributed networks, the Net is simultaneously connected to the whole and to the one. Mass customization is a system that allows a product or service to exist both as the sum of its component parts (e.g., all that's in the database) and as a particular product or service customized by the individual (such as CRAYON). By allowing consumers to pick and choose among component parts, a company can create more products at no extra cost, at the same time enhancing brand and building loyalty. Here are a few companies that are creating opportunities for consumers to build their own products in the Digital Estate:

- *Lombard Institutional Brokerage* in San Francisco uses the Net to allow personal computers to resemble the same terminal look and feel of traders at large investment houses. Customers can monitor their own portfolios, retrieve their own financial and corporate information from the brokerage databases, and use analytical tools supplied by the brokerage. Lombard projects that the company will be conducting 40 percent of its trades over the Net by the year 2000. Customers here do more than the brokerage houses' work, they create their own sets of tools and features so that they, in effect, become researchers and brokers.

- *AccountingNet* is the publisher of a communications and marketing network for the accounting industry on the Internet. The site features up-to-date news, continuing education, and progressive membership programs. AccountingNet offers a turnkey solution for its members, allowing them to create, edit, and modify online content. In addition to such features as an information desk, catalogs, class registration, a database of home pages, job and resume postings, and membership applications, the site also acts as a communications tool between CPAs and their state societies. Each state society has its own autonomy, while AccountingNet centralizes the system. As the technology develops, the site will add merchant services, a video-conferencing network, and international licensing agreements.

- *Internet Underground Music Archive* is taking advantage of the plummeting cost of production by posting digital audio tracks from unknown artists on its site. Electronic keyboards, mixers, and other recording equipment already permit musicians to record and edit material inexpensively themselves. The major problem has been distribution. Internet Underground aims to change that. Bands can not only produce and distribute their music online, they can also check out consumers' reactions and modify their efforts accordingly. For the consumer, the site offers an interesting preview and a chance to participate in the production of music. But for the musician, the site offers the opportunity to create, distribute, customize, and sell the product without giving up creative control.

Web Tips to Help Customers Help Themselves

If a company is going to enable its customers to create products and do work, it needs to supply the right kind of environment. The look and feel of a Web site as well as the quality of its functionality say everything to prospective customers. Companies can help customers help themselves by giving them the tools they need in a comfortable space.

1. *Keep it clean.* Image isn't everything on the Net, but it certainly counts for a lot. A functional Web site should avoid gratuitous displays of techno-tricks that clutter up the site. If graphics are important to the company business, use them. But if the customer has come to fill out a form or perform a search, don't slow them down by adding graphics simply because it can be done. In a world of excess like the Web, clean, well-considered sites assure visitors that the company has their best interests at heart.

2. *Keep it simple.* Avoid complex jargon, overwrought explanations, and confusing tangents. Always keep the customer's point-of-view in focus. Ask yourself, "What have they come here to do?" Then design a site that matches the answer. Make sure everything works the way it is supposed to, and be sure to provide instructions for using the site.

3. *Organize logically.* Go with the three-click rule: If users can't get to the core of the information they're looking for in three clicks, they'll abandon the search. It's a good rule of thumb. Web sites often start with a graphic cover page that links to a text-and-graphic cover page that links to mysterious internal pages, which link to subcategories which link to more links, etc. Organization is key. Standard information about the company, such as background, biographies, office address/phone/fax, and highlights are frequently collected under the "About" button. This is not, however, the appropriate place for a search function. Attention spans on the Net are short, information and services readily available, and customers have all the control. Think about how information and material can be logically arranged. Think about it from the user's point of view.

Web Tips to Help Customers Help Themselves *(cont.)*

4. *Interact with the customer.* Customers need to know that someone in the company is monitoring the site and cares about what they want. Use an e-mail response system that automatically sends a message acknowledging any e-mail sent by the customer. Post Frequently Asked Questions, commonly referred to as FAQs, so that users don't waste the company's time with repetitive questions and their own time waiting for a response when answers are already available. Take surveys and offer incentive/rewards to customers who are willing to participate.

5. *Provide customers with what they expect to find.* If a company sells ice cream offline, then it better have something about ice cream somewhere on its Web site. As the Web grows and certain standards of business etiquette, or Netiquette, emerge, one that tops the list is designing Web sites that match customer expectations. A customer who goes to a site like Encyclopedia Britannica expects to find not only the encyclopedia, but sophisticated search technology. Of course, it never hurts to exceed customer expectation by offering innovative services that enhance their experience on site. In the case of Britannica, audio and video options are value-added features entirely appropriate to the site.

6. *Let them know you are out there.* 'If you build it, they will come.' That may be so, but not if they don't know about it. Logical domain names such as www.disney.com are no guarantee that online customers will drop by. In addition to advertising on the Net and in other media, companies can guide customers to their sites by registering with search engines and by strategic linking with other companies. Also, do not ignore the power of home pages, e-mail newsletters, press releases, and company announcements. Do not insult the Net community by posting veiled ads in newsgroups and sending company employees into chats in order to draw traffic.

7. *Pay for talent and training.* No company wants to drop millions into an unproved medium. Ironically, that is precisely what companies are doing when they move to the Net on a shoestring budget. Poorly designed sites and untrained or unprepared staff members result in costly losses of potential revenue. Consumers are fairly tolerant of mistakes when they are convinced that a company is trying to learn. Customers will view a half-hearted site as an insulting waste of their time.

THE INTRANETWORKED ENTERPRISE

How information is distributed on the Net affects more than the relationship between consumer and company. Company intranets, or internal, Web-compatible company networks, are using the Internet to build enterprisewide networks. The benefits are compelling. It's inexpensive and it's global. The problem with using the

Internet is, of course, security. Companies may not mind customers accessing a database of their products, but they certainly can't afford to have outsiders hacking into the accounts and other sensitive internal information. The solution is an intranet, which uses a software firewall as a barrier, a trap door of sorts. Employees can venture out beyond the corporate wall, but outsiders can't come in without proper authorization.

Companies that adopted intranets early on have been learning what works and what doesn't. When intranets permeate the enterprise, this knowledge and experience will pay by developing a work force and a company strategy poised to push ahead at maximum speed.

Some companies link their intranets to the Internet, while others build them on top of existing closed networks. What distinguishes an intranet is its compatibility with Internet and World Wide Web protocols, such as TCP/IP. Whether connected or not, intranets are adopting the look and feel of the Web, a look and feel that companies like. One survey of 150 companies found that 23 percent had already implemented or planned to implement internal Web sites, while another 20 percent were thinking about it.[1] One reason that intranets are so popular is the ease with which workers can use them. With increased intranet participation, companies will experience the same enhancement of internal user control and customization of information that is taking place on the Net. By liberating the knowledge of the corporate databases and translating it into the common, user-friendly language of the Web, these companies are creating what I have termed the Intranetworked Enterprise.

SHARING THE INFORMATION

Hewlett-Packard has one of the largest private intranets in the world, with 140,000 hosts transmitting more than five terabytes of information a month, over 400 sites worldwide, 82,000 PCs, 23,000 Unix desktops, 6,000 servers, 70,000 Netscape Navigator desktops, 2,500 Web servers, and 170 Proxy/Caching Servers. According to the company's own internal case study, the deployment of intranets allows for greater organizational flexibility and created an explosion of information sharing among its employees.[2]

The corporate-wide intranet enables faster time to market, improved customer relationships, reduced cost structures, and better communication. The intranet is now HP's strategic computing platform, with all HP-distributed computing initiatives coalesced on the Web. HP is banking that its position in providing open systems and services for the industry will make it more flexible and competitive.

HP is using its intranet for a number of projects. Human Resources uses it, with a search engine, to distribute personnel policies and guidelines. COE (Common Operating Environment) is a distribution vehicle for client/server applications to more than 80,000 PCs throughout the company. With COE, employee desktop PCs are no longer exclusively personal but become elements of the PC COE system. Common PC applications such as word processing, spreadsheets, and presentation software are loaded from centralized servers, and the intranet allows the company to reduce the number of manufacturing design iterations from as many as eight to a single product. Now even change orders are done on the Web.

Another of the intranet applications, Electronic Sales Partner, delivers sales and product information from the divisions to the field. With ESP, interaction with customers has evolved from merely providing information to having time to listen to requirements and solve problems. This application uses a folder structure and full text search to provide a single source for all information, including data sheets, white papers, and competitive briefs. More than 4,000 sales reps can download and print over 10,000 different documents. A survey of selected users indicated that ESP was saving them an average of five hours of work a week. The savings in mail and printing costs are also substantial.

The HP intranet is a glimpse into the power of distributive thinking, particularly since it furnishes end users with more control over the information they need. The sales rep who needs a graphic can easily log on and get it. Office memos can be stored and searched online. According to CEO Lewis F. Platt, "HP's corporate culture has always encouraged open communication among

employees. But with the advent of our intranet, information sharing has taken off like never before."

While relatively few companies produce networks as part of
their core business, intranets are becoming an essential component for business in the Digital Estate. Other examples of intra-
networking include:

- *GameNet,* hosted by the graphics imaging company Idea Center,
  Inc., has set up an intranet for the gaming industry. GameNet is
  an electronic meeting place for hotels and suppliers to work out
  operational functions such as image creation, proofing, editing,
  electronic mail, and gaming information. They electronically
  collaborate to design and build necessary intra-gaming components for their operations.

- *Tyson Foods* has more than 100 remote sites worldwide and over
  5,000 employees using corporate computing capabilities for information access. It opted for a corporate intranet, complete
  with advertising from the company credit union. In addition to
  a phone database, the site features corporate policy manuals,
  news, updates, and product data. Remote site data ranges from
  maps and travel information to complete status reports on every
  workstation operating at remote locations.

- *SmartUtah* is a statewide intranet that networks every organization, business, and government agency in the state of Utah. The
  goal of the intranet is twofold: to increase efficiency in government operations and to increase citizen participation. State residents can renew their driver's licenses online, and parents can
  use the intranet to communicate with teachers. Another driver
  for the intranet was to attract industry to the state.

THE CONSUMER-CENTRIC NET

As the Net becomes a utility and hundreds of millions of people
get connected, there will be little choice for companies but to push
as much out to the Net as possible. This will include everything
from applications to product creation to services that enable customer customization. Customers will say when they will buy what,
providing manufacturers input so that they can create products on

demand. Customers will tell companies who they are, in great detail, in trade for the information or service they want.

With information appliances, smart cards, higher bandwidths, and easy access to interactive, highly specific areas of interest, companies will more and more be working for the consumers. The Digital Estate is consumer-centric, not company-centric because consumers have the ability to instantly click in and out of any site. The sooner companies learn how to engage their customer base on the Net, the better they will be able to enable them to do future work.

CONTEXT IS KING

Real estate listings, personals, canned goods, scuba gear, hotel reservations, magazines, legal advice, medical records, technical specifications, blue jeans, and college campuses all have one thing in common: they all are forms of content. Once it is digitized and moved onto the Net, any data becomes content, making almost any company doing business in the digital world of the Net a content provider.

This is sometimes an unsettling idea for industries used to thinking of their business in terms of merchandise, commodities, and transactions. Content, after all, has been the prime property of the media industry. Ironically, traditional content providers such as newspapers and magazines have a difficult time adjusting to the dynamics of a networked world, where the creation, storage, and distribution of digital content in an interactive environment transforms the value associated with that content. In the Digital Estate, it is context, not content, that determines value.

The problem is that content alone is almost useless in an internetworked environment, especially if the content is available more readily through another medium, such as a magazine delivered monthly straight to the mailbox. In this respect, the words on the page make up the content. On the Net, however, not only are the words important, but also the associations surrounding the words. When, where, and how the words appear are key factors that determine the content's value. Context is the combination of all of these factors: time, place, relevant content, and technology.

Context is king in the Digital Estate because context takes into account a network of surrounding issues and elements. Context is fluid, malleable, responsive, interactive. So is the Net. Context is also the key to rethinking the traditional role of content providers and static notions of content.

PUTTING CONTENT INTO CONTEXT

Learning to think of products and services—as opposed to words and images—as content is the first hurdle for content providers in the Digital Estate, particularly nontraditional content providers. The second major obstacle is learning to separate the traditional notions of what constitutes content with what constitutes *successful* content on the Net.

Traditional content is static, like the words on a printed page. Once those words are printed, a reader can read, skim, or ignore them, but the reader cannot change them. More importantly, static content exists only in a one-way relationship to the user. Content to user. What the user does as a result of the content affects the content provider only indirectly, if at all.

Interactive content is dynamic, inviting the user to participate in the creation. User interaction may be as simple as filling out a form for real-time, relevant results or as substantial as participating in a global, interactive, multimedia discussion group. However, a page containing everything anyone ever needed to know about restaurants in a city, including video clips and photos, is not totally interactive if the customer must go offline to make a reservation. Suppose, however, that the service provider also includes reservation capability, seating charts with time availability, and automatically recalls where you sat on your last visits or what kind of seating you generally prefer, dietary preferences, and special offers for you. It then adds a breadth of context that makes the experience total. It becomes *usefully* interactive.

The Web is inherently interactive, but many companies have trouble grasping the implications of how interactivity changes the dynamics between consumers and companies. These companies act as if posting an e-mail address return address field constitutes interactivity. Functions such as searchable databases, e-mail, and purchase orders are expected in an internetworked world, as were voice mail, 800 numbers, and three-way calling capabilities in the pre-connectivity era. These services quickly will go from interactive services to fundamental consumer demands. While they may be technically interactive functions, they do not really enhance the interactive experience in and of themselves. Context is needed.

Content in context is the heart of what makes an online experience truly interactive and it represents a vast array of options depending on the design of the industry and company that uses it (see Table 12-1). Interactivity is extended to include more than communication because the user's participation isn't just a service; it is part of a business plan to outsource resources. Content in context is a way of looking at a business on the Web from the user's point of view. In addition to the core attraction of the base information, context provides a wide-angle view of related information and services, anticipating the needs of the user.

CREATING THE CONTEXT

An easy way to build a context for interactive content is to think like a spider and build a web around the core element that motivates the content. After defining its endgame (that vision thing)— knowing what it wants to be in relationship to its customers and in relationship to its competitors—a company needs to chart the potential networks made possible by the Net.

For example, a scuba diving school in the Caribbean might expand its Web site to include tourist information about the islands. By forming strategic partnerships with local and regional partners, the scuba school could help customers book travel and accommodations. The school could also sell merchandise, sponsor chats, and offer online tutorials. By extending the scope of its core interest in selling scuba lessons to visitors coming to the island, this company could build a reputation as the premier scuba school in the Caribbean and pull interested customers into taking a vacation. The Net makes forming such extended networks not only possible, but also practical.

Companies of the Digital Estate are discovering the potential of creating dynamic contexts for their businesses in an internet-

TABLE 12-1. Context in the Digital Estate

CONTENT PROVIDER	STATIC CONTENT	CONTENT IN CONTEXT
1. *Real estate.* The content provided by real estate companies is the information about the properties they are trying to sell.	• Listing of available properties • Standard components, such as number and size of rooms • Special features such as enclosed carport or appliances • Photographs of the property • Contact or agency information	• 3D model of the property • Interactive maps of surrounding area, searchable by selected radius, with links to specific sites such as grocery stores, dry cleaners, churches, schools, the post office, restaurants • City facts and highlights • Direct, interactive access to realtors • Interactive moving and packing resources • Properties presented based on your current environment
2. *Travel.* The content provided by the travel industry includes both information and booking services.	• List of transportation and accommodations options either through a primary business, such as Hertz, Delta, or Hilton, or through a broad-based service such as a travel agent • Searchable database • Booking facilities • Company and contact information	• Personalized trip planners • Mileage and gas estimators • Air miles calculator, tied to individuals' frequent flyer programs; automatic suggestions to save money • Restaurant and nightlife guides, including menus and reservations booking • Interactive, multimedia tourist brochures • Automatic proposals based on where you have been
3. *Grocery Stores.* The content provided by grocery stores is both the product on the shelf and the information pertaining to it.	• Catalog of items in stock • Searchable database • Online ordering and delivery • Company information	• Price comparisons • Product information such as unit price, calorie, fat, ingredients • Criteria calculators including price, food groups, types of product, total calorie count, etc. • Electronic coupons • Online specials • Smart agent check-out racks • Preselection of groceries based on past purchases and personal dietary needs

TABLE 12-1. Context in the Digital Estate *(cont.)*

Content Provider	Static Content	Content in Context
4. *Health Care.* The content provided by the health care industry includes records, research, general information, and medical services.	• List of health care providers and health care institutions • Emergency information • Physician profiles • Health tips and pamphlets • Calendar of community events, such as blood drives or TB tests • Searchable database for medical desk reference	• Community chats, such as a cancer group or an AIDS chat • Bill analysis function • Direct insurance filing • Drugstore orders and delivery • Personalized reference area that updates and delivers only news selected by patient • Preliminary check-in • Booking for appointments • Wellness community program
5. *Insurance.* The content provided by insurance companies includes policy information in all areas of coverage.	• Agent information and locator • Policy brochures • Safety and health tips • Online request forms with an e-mail return estimate • Options database • Financial estimator	• Claims submission form • Insurance portfolio organizer • Comparative rates • Customized package deals • Direct links to affiliates, such as doctors, auto repair shops, financial consultants • Centralized disaster relief efforts • Bill payment options
6. *Fundraising.* The content provided by fundraising organizations includes information about the aims of the organization and how funds are used.	• Organization information • Lists of upcoming events • Latest news • Solicitation materials • Online pledge cards • Testimonials	• Interactive auctions • Home page awareness campaigns that get participants to post ribbons or other materials on their own sites • Chats, bulletin boards, and featured online speakers • Micropayment donations • E-mail reminder notices • Tax deduction calculators, based on knowledge of your personal, financial situation

worked world. Using strategies suited to their core content, these companies are finding that the interactive nature of their content in context transforms what they ultimately do. Here are four strategies for putting content into context:

1. Atmosphere
2. Community
3. Service
4. Product

1. Atmosphere: In the Mood

Creating the right atmosphere is essential for conducting business online, even for companies unaccustomed to having their customers in their brick and mortar buildings. A car manufacturer doesn't need to worry that potential buyers will make a trip to Detroit to check out the latest model minivan. The dealers have been responsible for creating the right atmosphere for their communities. Even so, the automotive alleys throughout the thousands of towns across the country rarely have distinguishing features. They are generally one-story buildings big enough to showcase a few models inside with offices lining the walls. The object of the architecture is to stay out of the way so that the buyer can concentrate on the automobile. That's fair enough offline.

On the Net, not only does the manufacturer need to create an inviting site, but also local dealers, to avoid disintermediation, must also present an inviting and dynamic online atmosphere that gives customers what they want. Since customers can't actually test drive a car online, it is even more important for the site to take advantage of the interactivity inherent in the medium.

As virtual reality modeling technologies develop, dealers will be able to take an online customer out for a virtual spin. Meantime, the options include comparison shopping search capabilities, interactive models that let the user click on a feature of the car to find out more about it, online loan applications, chats and bulletin boards featuring an online mechanic, e-mail newsletters, the ability to select and piece features together to design and order a new car, interactive road maps, and direct, interactive access to other owners of models of interest. These types of elements transform raw data into dynamic content, and they can build an online atmosphere appropriate to the product.

- *Ragu* used to be just a spaghetti sauce. On the Net it is a legend, or rather Mama Cucina and her kitchen are. The site is anything but a product information area, although information is, of course, provided. Rather the site is designed around Mama Cucina, and more closely resembles a soap opera than an advertisement. Visitors can check out Mama's kitchen and living room, browse through Mama's cookbook, learn Italian, win prizes, take a virtual tour of Italy, talk to Mama, chat at the Pizza parlor, and even follow the onsite soap opera, "As the Lasagna Bakes." And all the talk about food whets one's appetite.
- *Valvoline* doesn't promote motor oil on the Net. Instead, it focuses on the engines that make the motor run. The company features information on stock car racing events, with daily standings, images, movies, and a history of auto racing. Graphics make it look like a garage, with icons built into the fabric of the main image. For racing and car enthusiasts, the only thing missing is the grease.
- *Lego* is a good example of how a company can build a context for its product in a digital environment by sticking to its roots. The company created an electronic environment that was fun, full of bells and whistles, rotating tots, and clicking bricks. The idea was to have children set up shop on their own Lego home page made out of Lego blocks. Little Lego icons abound.

2. COMMUNITY: THE LOCAL FORECAST

When millions of new users rushed onto the World Wide Web, some cautionary visionaries worried that people would lose touch with the real world. Locked away in dark rooms mesmerized by the eerie glow of the computer, cyberjunkies would spend hours roaming aimlessly around the Internet. So the fears ran. It ended up that most people go online to communicate and interact with others. Community is a powerful aspect of Net life, as previously discussed. The Net is a vast umbrella circumscribing millions of smaller communities. Just as traditional businesses have found ways to integrate their products and services into geographic communities, so businesses online must seek new ways to tap into the need for communities on the Net.

The difference is that, on the Net, a business can actually *create* a community. By identifying the common ground among its customers—a hobby, an ailment, a product, a profession, a mindset, or anything else—businesses can use their sites to build community in one of two ways. They can aggregate and create community-specific content. The Space Camp Community could include links to NASA, interactive games, space-related school projects, a space travel calculator, a space camp competition, and a rocket design contest. The possibilities are almost endless!

A Web presence can also be used as a public park, a logical meeting place. For example, Toyota created tangent sites, linked to the company's home page, that operate as independent areas. The Hub and *Women's World Weekly* offer relevant general content and interactive options in the form of chats and bulletin boards, with no particular emphasis on automobiles.

About the only limit to building a community online is the imagination and insight needed to see an opportunity and take it. Here is a sampling of other online communities:

- *Miami City Web* offers visitors language options, restaurant and entertainment information, classifieds, neighborhood maps, public transportation information, merchant listings and coupons, and a hotel/motel directory. The site also offers local residents and businesses a home page hosting service.

- *AtHand,* hosted by Pacific Bell, is a search service listing every business in the state of California. The service uses descriptive content from travel guides, local magazines, and syndicated news services, which supply context-specific advertising. For example, a user interested in mountain biking in Northern California can locate stores, restaurants, equipment, and promotions in a specific area, in addition to accessing product reviews, safety tips, discussion groups, trail specifications, and other relevant information.

3. SERVICE: WHO HAS TIME FOR HASSLES?

On the Net, with the end user always in control, *clickitis*, the previously described propensity of users to click away at any moment, represents a significant challenge to Digital Estate businesses. One way to keep customers on site and interested is to provide them with a service unique to the environment. Certain industries, such as travel and real estate, which have always been service-oriented, have a built-in advantage (whether they take it or not) on the Net: Their customer base is information-hungry. Information on the Net, however, is so ubiquitous that you need to supply additional incentives to attract consumers. Content alone will not do it.

By building a context centered around service, Digital Estate companies are finding that it is not information that consumers can't get enough of, but service, specifically services that permit them the greatest amount of freedom to locate what they want, and when and where they want it. Technologies such as smart agents, cookies, search engines, interactive mapping, and direct database access are invaluable and relatively inexpensive tools for creating a service context. The key is to identify services that correspond to the core business. Travel agents are a good example. The business of a travel agent is to book travel and accommodation: the more bookings, the more profits.

On the Net, individual users can go directly to airlines to book seats, to hotels to book rooms, to car rental services to book cars, to museums and restaurants to book reservations, and so on. Of course, they can perform these functions offline as well. The value of the traditional travel agency rested in its ability to aggregate information that was not readily available to the public. An interactive agency, on the other hand, must compete with the very companies that it aggregates. The only way to circumvent disintermediation is to make accessing information easier and cheaper through the agency site. Ironically, on the Net, giving the customers keys to the databases so that they, in effect, do the work of the agent, is considered a premium service. Thinking in context requires that the agency think in component parts. An interactive agency can create a customized package with little extra effort because customers pick and choose exactly what they want from available databases, which they may then book directly.

A look at some nontraditional services demonstrates the wide range of possibilities for creating services in the Digital Estate.

- *Multex Systems,* which delivers financial analyst research electronically through third-party distributors, such as Reuters and Bloomberg, added delivery directly to consumers via the Internet. MultexNet permits subscribers to retrieve full-text analyst reports for a $150 per month user fee for unlimited access. Though the service is marketed to brokerages and institutions, anyone willing to pay can have access. The content of the site is the database. The context is making the content available through direct delivery.

- *Thomas Cook* extended its world-travel business into a new arena with the addition of The Business Centre at Heathrow. The airport cybercafe and Internet Centre features full-service, modem-linked PCs, a library of CD-ROMs that may be checked out for free, and, of course, complimentary drinks and snacks. The Centre charges a minimal rate for online access based on time.

- *DataMatters,* a U.K. Internet service provider, teamed up with a local hospital to provide its customers with an organ donor registry. New Heart New Start program represents an opportunity for Internet businesses to give something back to the Net. Public service opportunities abound on the Net since the primary goal of almost all organizations, in addition to raising money, is to educate the public by getting their messages out.

4. PRODUCT: WHEN ONLY THE BEST WILL DO

Finally, what is the best strategy for building context around a quality product? Labels announcing new and improved do not translate well in a digital environment where everything is show, not tell. Demonstration has always been a powerful tool, but the Net makes it much easier to manipulate.

- *Home Improvement Encyclopedia* uses the look and feel of the Web as an interface for its CD-ROM. It's a natural fit. Using

Netscape to navigate the data on the disk, especially a reference disk, made the product more accessible by converting the interface to a common standard.

- *TalkCity,* a content studio operated by LiveWorld Productions, creates and operates original Internet programming focused on community and audience participation. The product in this case is the production of original content for companies looking to build digital communities. TalkCity debuted with more than 100 scheduled chats monitored by conference hosts. LiveWorld's strategy is to use the advertising-supported TalkCity to establish the company's reputation as "a leading provider of quality community based services on the Internet." LiveWorld expects to release new, original content on an ongoing basis.

INFORMATION WITH MORE MEANING

Researchers at MIT's Media Laboratory's News in the Future consortium developed a program called PLUM (Peace Love and Understanding Machine), a news augmentation system developed to provide greater meaning to news stories about natural disasters. The problem, as identified by MIT, was that when people thought of personalized news, they most often thought of filtered news, selecting stories of particular interest to an individual. They concluded that personalized news could have a different meaning, called augmentation, by which stories would be placed in context that would make them more relevant and engaging to readers.

In a story about a disaster, such as an earthquake in Indonesia, readers in New York would receive information comparing the quake to the worst earthquakes in U.S. history, while readers in Buenos Aires would receive similar statistics relating to Argentina, and so on. The system analyzes a story, extracts the facts, then taps databases to automatically generate annotations appropriate to specified geographic communities. Next, it hyperlinks the annotations to the original story. A reader triggers the context by clicking on highlighted words within the story. The Media Lab chose news about disasters because such stereotypically bad news partly shapes people's understanding of distant countries.

Technology such as this could one day be used for education, daily news, searches on various subjects, or providing dramatically deeper "information sessions" for individuals. In an internetworked world, the planet will seem to shrink, and information availability will be limitless. As time is increasingly compressed, context will become even more essential. Whether the subject matter is richer real estate and travel information or providing augmented news that increases people's understanding of each other's environments, context in the Digital Estate will give information a totally new meaning.

LIVING INSIDE THE NET

Part of the approach of companies doing business in the Digital Estate is how they think about living and working in a virtual environment and how they deal with it. They tend to mirror many of their business practices to the fluid nature of the Net itself, and have aggressive perspectives on time, collaboration, the prospects of electronic commerce, and the coming explosive use of digital money.

Given the high speed at which things happen on the Net, leaders of the Digital Estate live in what is referred to in the industry as *Net Time*. Any company that cannot adapt to this pace can be in serious trouble trying to compete in the environment. Net years make dog years look slow. A deal that takes six months to consummate in a traditional business environment might take six weeks from start to finish in the Digital Estate. A rough calculation of Net Time is ten to one, or ten calendar years for one Net Year.

While complex technological and infrastructure issues must be resolved before Net Time begins to operate at full capacity, Digital Estate companies are already thinking ahead. As they learn to quickly adapt to changes, to mimic the Net environment, and to think collaboratively, these companies are building a corporate tolerance for life in the digital fast lane. Thinking fast on the Net is not a gimmick or clever character trait; it is a matter of survival. Just as divers experience the bends when ascending without adequate preparation, companies unaccustomed to the rapid pace of the Net may find it increasingly more difficult to get up to speed as time goes by. In the Digital Estate, learning how to adapt to this new environment daily strengthens their ability to thrive.

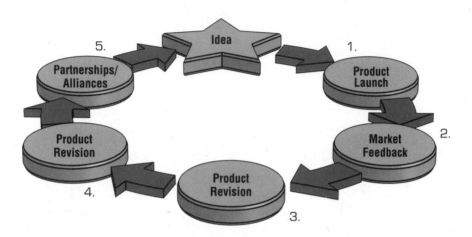

FIGURE 13-1

VIRTUALTHINK

Smart agents are a technology capable of learning, but they can also teach businesses how to think virtually. Thinking like an agent means translating everything on the Net into bit-sized data. We live and breathe in a physical world, and the Net is not a natural habitat. It evolved from a principle that dates back to the nineteenth century when Charles Babbage set out to build an Analytical Engine by adapting a logic system created by his contemporary, George Boole. The idea was to turn data into digits by translating numbers and words into two categories: 0s and 1s. These digits are the stuff upon which virtual worlds are built.

The key to virtuality of the Net is that, once data is digitized, it can be disseminated and assembled in an infinite variety of ways. Thinking smart, in this context, is learning to see the parts as separate from the whole. When Hollywood needed to insert Tom Hanks, as Forrest Gump, into contemporary historical moments, it did so by first thinking of the records of these events as virtual documents. A video of John F. Kennedy delivering a speech from the Oval Office is not just a series of individual frames moving through a camera. On the digital level, each individual frame is also a complex compilation of bits of information. By rearranging and altering the bits, Hollywood seamlessly integrated Hanks into the original footage, so that he *was* virtually shaking hands with President Kennedy or playing football for the Crimson Tide.

Digital Estate companies are taking the same principles and applying them to products and services. This kind of smart thinking radically alters how and what businesses can do because it locates value at the bit level. In the Digital Estate, the sum of the parts almost always exceeds the value of the whole. The Net is like a vast set of millions of Lego pieces, and it is up to each company what to build. What the Lego masters of the Digital Estate have found is that the only limit to the kinds of transactions that can take place on the Net is the ability to concentrate on finding new ways to increase the value of the parts.

THE COLLABORATIVE NET

Smart agents work by making connections. Good connections are reinforced and grow stronger, while bad connections grow weak and dissolve. The designers of artificial intelligence are accustomed to thinking about how thinking works. Neural and digital intelligence systems comprise elaborate combinations of networks that are themselves complex structures that can respond to positive and negative feedback. Thinking is a process that requires both collaborative associations (cats and dogs are animals) and competitive associations (the cat is not a hat).

It is not necessary, however, to hire a cognitive engineer from MIT to demonstrate the importance of simultaneous partnering and competing, or *coopetition*, in the Digital Estate. No matter where you look in the Net environment, companies are partnering with one another.

Companies have formed partnerships in the Digital Estate for many reasons. One reason is that with such a fast-growth market, the make-or-buy decision is replaced by the benefits of simple teaming, creating win-win scenarios in compressed time spans. Also, the I-Way can be a lonely road. Finally, for some companies it simply seemed like a good idea at the time. As the leaders of the Digital Estate all try to climb the same huge, uncharted mountain, being tied together in teams seems to help each on their way to the peak, at least psychologically, if not in reality.

The necessity and desire for collaboration should continue, because the centralization of product, technology, and ideas don't work well in the environment. There are simply too many people with too many good ideas to buy them all up. The Net thrives on grassroots collaboration. Similarly, there are as many kinds of collaborations as there are companies to form them.

There are three basic partnering schemes for collaborating on the Net:

1. Big Company–Big Company
2. Big Company–Small Company
3. Small Company–Small Company

COMBOS IN THE DIGITAL ESTATE

BIG COMPANY–BIG COMPANY

- *Upside:* Established brands and product lines can be leveraged; efficiencies in scale; can be standard-setting; well-resourced.
- *Downside:* Speed to market may not be competitive; product may not be relevant compared to new offerings by others; internal politics may slow or compromise product; knowledge-sharing difficulties.

BIG COMPANY–SMALL COMPANY

- *Upside to Big:* Gain of market knowledge; fast-moving team; potential new product line.
- *Upside to Small:* Infrastructure; working capital; market muscle; credibility.
- *Downside to Big:* Internal negative reaction; product and product team conflict; culture clash.

- *Downside to Small:* Time-consuming; political; bureaucratic; potentially smothering; culture clash.

  SMALL COMPANY–SMALL COMPANY
- *Upside:* Same language spoken; low cost; fulfillment of each other's need; easy to accomplish; speed of operation and cycle time similar.
- *Downside:* Lack of long-term, formal structure; can get ugly when money flows; may not add to scalability.

In addition to scale, there are a number of reasons that companies in the Digital Estate partner with one another. Technology is a prime motive, as are brand enhancement and superior content. Many of the largest companies that are traditional competitors are curbing their competitive instincts to build a viable infrastructure and to push through advantageous standards for the future. Alliances and consortia, such as the Alliance for Converging Technologies and CommerceNet, demonstrate the power of partnering in the Digital Estate. Here are some examples of collaboration in the Digital Estate:

- Consumer goods giant Procter & Gamble and Yahoo! jointly launched an Internet promotional campaign and introduced a new method of advertising payment, based on how many consumers were referred from Yahoo! to the P&G brands.

- A group of 40 chemical and agricultural companies contributed $5 million to create TCP/IP-based networks to cut costs, as well as inventories, to improve performance flow among manufacturers, retailers, and distributors. Subscribers tap into a secure Web site called PowerAg that provides information on regulatory and industry issues. The network includes electronic data interchange (EDI) and electronic funds transfer (EFT).

- NetCount Chairman Paul Grand decided his Web tracking software company needed a partner to be a market leader. So it teamed with Price Waterhouse, positioning NetCount as the accounting firm of the Internet.

- Software.com Inc. and Accordance Corp. merged to offer Internet messaging services for everything from small business to large corporations. Software.com had served small and medium-sized organizations, while Accordance served the high end of the market.

- Oracle Corp, the developer of database software, and VeriFone Inc., a maker of credit-card swiping systems, joined to build a secure Web payment system for businesses and consumers. The combination of Oracle's WebServer software and VeriFone's secure payment software became the first payment-enabling Web server available in the market.

- When Kodak decided it would bet on people trading photos over the Internet, based on the fact that 73 percent of current Kodak customers mail photos to others, it partnered with Microsoft Corp., Hewlett-Packard Co., and Live Picture Software to produce a faster image file format without extra computer memory or additional equipment.

- Silicon Alley-based iVillage and Silicon Valley-based Electric Classifieds collaborated on the iVillage Web site for parents. By using Electric Classified's personal service Match.com, iVillage was able to add a new dimension to its parents' information services. Visitors to the ParentSoup, potentially single parents, are offered the option of meeting up with like-minded people by being sent to match.com. For its part, Electric Classified's maintained the ParentSoup brand throughout the portions of its services that ParentSoup visitors roamed through.

- Polaroid Corp., in conjunction with Fox Broadcasting Co., launched a steamy soap opera on the Net called Polaroid Place at the Fox-World site on the Web. The online serial provided narrative written by Fox. Users could see photos of the characters and link to Polaroid's site. The objective for Polaroid was to increase traffic to its site. The online soap was an extension of a $40 million corporate ad campaign. Online serials drive viewers. Once users got to the Polaroid site, they found games and frequently challenging brain teasers. Winners received Polaroid products.

- *Virtual City*, a New York-based magazine backed by *Newsweek*, hooked up with Internet navigation company Excite in a trade arrangement: *Virtual City* agreed to carry a dozen pages of Web site reviews from Excite in trade for *Virtual City* ad banners on Excite's home page. Those ads link to increase subscriptions for the publication, as well as link to the publication's Web site, to increase its traffic.

- Sun's sophisticated Java technology allowed applets, or miniprograms, to be moved throughout the Web, increasing animation capabilities and facilitating business-to-business information transportation. The program was widely acclaimed and licensed and incorporated into products by companies such as Netscape, Apple, and IBM. When total market acceptance of Sun's Java technology reached mass proportions, Microsoft agreed also to license and incorporate it into future products.

Partnering is part of the fabric of the Net, the most open of open systems. When a company electronically links its consumers to another company, it is considered a service and is viewed positively. This is all part of the virtual dynamic that makes the Net tick. For all its promise, however, the Net could never become more than an elaborate communications network if it weren't for one simple fact: A digital network is the ideal environment for digital transactions.

DIGITAL MONEY

To Digital Estate companies, it is not a matter of whether, but how fast, virtual commerce will take off. It is a collaboration of enormous proportions involving global cooperation among companies in different as well as in competing industries. The players in this new economy share a firm conviction that electronic commerce *will* happen, that there *will* be electronic forms of currency, that security issues *will* be resolved, and that consumers *will* learn to adapt to online transactions. Building consumer confidence is a key factor in pushing electronic commerce forward. One of the most difficult challenges facing the first generation of businesses on the Net is to discover how the advent of virtual commerce changes the relationships between businesses and their customers.

Here's a look at what is enticing consumers to use the Net to manage, spend, and invest their money—and how the Digital Estate is responding.

MANAGING MONEY DIGITALLY

Security First Network Bank in Pineville, Kentucky, was the first bank in the United States designed to do business entirely through the Net. The virtual bank quickly attracted more than 2,000 customers with no advertising, low operating costs, and its user-friendly interface for the PC. After more than a decade of dabbling in home banking options, banks are finding that the Net is ideally suited for pushing home banking into the mainstream. Branch banking will slowly disappear as ATM kiosks expand their services and banks aggressively push their online options. Like the ATM, home banking is a service that banks can't afford *not* to offer. Customers and businesses will quickly take for granted the ability to bank from anywhere at any time. No longer hostage to the institution in a particular place, digital consumers will shop around for great deals and good service. And if they can't find them with the traditional banks, they'll go elsewhere.

Home banking ultimately will help change perceptions about how everyone thinks of money, which can affect all forms of commerce. While most of the online applications mimic the routine procedures of balancing accounts, transferring funds, and applying for loans, the advantage of home banking over traditional banking is the control, the instant access, it gives the customer. The long-term advantage that home banking offers to the growth and development of virtual commerce is the extent to which it helps change human behavior. As people get comfortable with online transactions, businesses that do not offer online options will find their customer bases dwindling.

An interesting side note to the increase in electronic banking is the range of new opportunities for providing turnkey systems for banks that want to add Internet transaction capabilities. BankSite, operated by the Forms Group, a direct marketing firm in Scottsdale, Arizona, provides banks on a tight budget with Internet banking services that allow banks to individually brand their services.

The start-up fee of $500 and the monthly fees of $150 are an inexpensive alternative to the thousands of dollars it costs to set up and maintain a Web site internally. When companies think fast and smart, they can anticipate profitable collaborations and create business opportunity where there was once none.

SPENDING DIGITAL MONEY

Just as home banking is basically about managing money digitally, a new industry is growing that enables businesses and consumers to spend their digital money. Not surprisingly, the competition is fierce among companies to come up with the best formula for transporting value from A to B. As companies such as DigiCash, First Virtual, CyberCash, and NetCash work through the issues of privacy and standards, online transactions are poised to take off. One British survey found that 81.9 percent of respondents expressed a willingness to use digital money on the Internet, while 8.8 percent had a negative attitude toward doing so, including a mere 2 percent who said they would never use it.[1] Survey responses indicate that 18.5 percent have used money on the Internet at least once, mainly credit cards (43.9 percent), DigiCash experimental ecash (26.8 percent), and First Virtual (12.2 percent). A more titillating aspect of the survey is that most of the respondents were university students. Their eagerness to buy online had less to do with traditional demographic considerations, such as gender, education, or financial status, than it did with the fact that these students were accustomed to instant access created by virtual environments, including television, gaming, and the Internet. It simply did not occur to them to think any other way. Where the Interactive Generation leads, the rest of the population will follow not far behind.

Most businesses are likely to take the conservative high road on money issues. Because it isn't yet certain which electronic payment systems will eventually carry the day, many companies are adopting a wait-and-see attitude. Leaders in the Digital Estate, however, are more than willing to take the risk of adopting a standard that may or may not make it because it gives them the opportunity to learn the ins and outs of dealing with instant commerce.

There are certain moves a company can make to circumvent the battle for electronic payment systems. First, they can allow payments through as many channels as possible by opening merchant accounts with each of the leading payment system companies. The earlier they do so the better, since most offer attractive deals to gain new business. Companies can also do homework to keep current on what is working for other companies, and they can seek advice from qualified sources. The Web makes it possible for anyone to contact, question, and research any company online. Thousands of articles about who's doing what and when are available. They are written by professors and graduate students, consultants and analysts, hobbyists, and the heaviest hitters in the game.

Investing Digital Money

In the 1980's, Charles Schwab, Inc. played David to the Merrill-Lynch Goliath. By offering cheaper investment costs and going after the small change of the average investor, Schwab tapped into the lucrative market of investment-minded middle America. The Net, however, represents a serious threat to both the Davids and Goliaths of the financial world.

The Net makes it possible for any individual with a PC and a modem to research, get quotes, access databases and company profiles, and place an order directly on the Net. One example that demonstrates the range of online opportunities for investing is Wit Capital, whose fast thinking founder, Andrew Klein, took the IPO for his three-year-old microbrewery, Spring Street, straight to the Net. This first-ever Internet IPO raised $1.6 million from 3,500 investors. The success of the first offer has prompted the company to go for another online stock offering of $3.3 million. Klein followed up this success by getting SEC approval for Wit-Trade, an online trading mechanism that bypasses brokers and commissions altogether. Company clients that hope to follow in Spring Street's footsteps will pay fees and transaction charges for participation in the Wit-Trade digital stock exchange.

Another example, with a slightly different slant, is the story of Guardian Insurance Financial Services, whose stock went from 2

1/8 to 6 points in only a couple of weeks for no apparent reason. A press release issued by the company attributed their gain to a favorable review by an electronic newsletter, the Waco Kid Hot Stocks Forum. This story is a testament to the fact that news travels fast and far on the Net.

Not surprisingly, investing is taking off on the Web. Investing money has everything to do with acquiring and analyzing information, and the Net is the ultimate tool for this kind of acquisition. Timing is everything. On the Web, much of what is available to professional brokers is now available to anyone. Disclosure Inc., headquartered in Bethesda, Maryland, is the leading provider of global company information and is available online. Disclosure provides reproduction services to the SEC and maintains its own unique, 26-year archive of historical SEC filings. It also operates the SEC's three public reference rooms and is a member of the project team that developed EDGAR (Electronic Data Gathering, Analysis, and Retrieval), the SEC's electronic filing system. Other such services are showing up in increasing numbers on the Web.

Like home banking and electronic payment systems, digital stock exchanges will revolutionize how people make, move, and spend money. This change will create new opportunities for those who can anticipate the needs of a world without walls. The Net brings about another change as well. Money will get smarter, transactions will be faster, and consumers and companies will take control over their own transactions. As the mechanisms that will push instant commerce toward critical mass fall into place, fast companies in the Digital Estate are preparing for the reality of tapping into a market of hundreds of millions of consumers. They don't have the time to wait and see what they already know is happening.

THE CHALLENGE OF KEEPING PACE

No one can predict with any certainty the details of electronic commerce in the distant future. Net Time, however, ensures that it will be a radical departure from today's industry norms. Time and space can be so compressed in the Digital Estate that everything becomes instant, including supply and demand.

Keeping pace with these changes will be challenge enough for any company. Thinking fast and thinking smart is the combination that counts. As more and more companies look at themselves in terms of what and who they connect, who they work with, and how they fit in an internetworked world, they will have to rethink their role in this virtual environment.

COMPETING AT GROUND ZERO

There is a joke told commonly in IT circles:

Question: "How could the world be created in just seven days?"
Answer: "There was no installed base to deal with."

For CEOs, this strikes a raw nerve, especially having had to transition their companies through the shift to open and distributed computing. In the Digital Estate, it is the raw nerve of CEOs that is exposed, as they grapple with how to transition to an internetworked world, where thousands of new companies, with no legacy technology or business to contend with, come directly at their core business, one piece at a time.

The challenge for these executives is how to maintain and grow the core business, while entering a new arena, where a simple brand extension might not be enough. Some mistake the Internet for simply a new distribution mechanism, implying that it is a one-way medium, while it is actually a two-way, communications medium.

Since new leaders of the Digital Estate are not dealing with an installed base of anything, they often play to this strength. For example, while established companies create relatively small, New Media departments to study brand extensions and manage the interactive environment, Digital Estate leaders devote *all* their energy, resource, manpower, and development—virtually all of their bandwidth—to the growth of their online, interactive business. These companies even anticipate the sometimes predictable moves (or lack of moves) of the larger companies in this environment.

This is the dilemma at Ground Zero, where the Digital Estate companies act as if a nuclear bomb has gone off and all the business activities are reset to zero, which is where they all recently started anyway. As stated earlier, this presents one of the most perplexing challenges in the Digital Estate: How does an established company transition itself to compete in the interactive environment, when its biggest customers and core business don't seem to depend on it? It's the age-old issue of tactics vs. strategy. With pressures of producing strong results next quarter and increasingly higher shareholder expectations, this corporate tear could be the undoing of many.

Oftentimes within large companies the new media individuals and departments are viewed as eccentrics, part of Research and Development, or just plain outsiders. The new media agents rarely carry significant, internal political muscle and aren't necessarily allowed to tamper with the core brands. By default, many end up proposing and executing brand enhancement strategies.

In larger companies, many middle-level executives focus on rising within the ranks, primarily by building on the current mode of operation. While maintaining the status quo, building on the current mode of operation, and generating predictable investments and returns are all very good for the rising middle managers and executives, they don't necessarily position companies to compete in the interactive environment. So while the brands are under siege by the companies not so restrained in this digital environment, a new internal political structure is threatening the status quo power structure.

To compete effectively in this environment, companies need to level set their approach to the business. Because the Net creates a new environment with different rules and economics, many companies are finding that the best way to compete is to detach the interactive operations from the core business traditions and processes. When carried to the extreme, this allows the interactive group to grow and flourish, creating new products that may even end up competing with the company's core products.

ENTER THE WEBMASTER

In the 70s, the IS department ruled, with total control of the huge mainframes in glass houses. The 1980s brought what some would call companywide, technological anarchy, as the PC revolution took the power from IS departments and placed it in the hands of individuals and business units. Then along came the client-server 1990s, with Local Area Networks, Wide Area Networks, and the movement to network-centric computing. Wanting not to relive the past, IS departments and business units began working together, sometimes even harmoniously, in a mutually beneficial crusade to deploy technology to achieve business objectives.

Then along came the Net and the World Wide Web, causing a different kind of turmoil within the corporate walls: This technological revolution affects the core business. It allows companies to seek new revenue streams, not reduce costs. It doesn't initially seem to enable core business practices, it threatens to replace them. With its TCP/IP, HTML, and friendly graphical interfaces, it doesn't immediately become a natural fit into the mission-critical IS environment, or at the business unit with all eyes on next quarter's results.

Out of this need emerged a new company function, that of Webmaster, the CIO for the 21st Century. Initially, companies tapped individuals who either showed a high interest in kicking off the company's Net presence, or who they figured could get the job done. The positions quickly evolved into the role of:

- Formulating a company's web strategy.
- Interfacing with numerous departments across the corporation to determine what content would appear.
- Originating and assuming responsibility for the technology of servers, architecture, Internet connections, and various other networking aspects.
- Driving HTML coding.
- Checking out new Net technology.
- Keeping the CEO apprised of the company's standing within the Net community.

Webmasters can come from various places, ranging from mar-keting to IS departments. As the Webmaster role evolves, estab-lished companies will be challenged in how to assimilate the func-tions within the corporation, since most of them of them don't report into the IS department. The growth of new roles in the Dig-ital Estate, such as that of Webmaster, offers established compa-nies a foundation from which to compete at Ground Zero. Some-times, though, these New Media leaders are viewed by others within the corporation as irrelevant, blue sky, revenue drains rather than as the heroes of the next generation.

DEFENDING THE HILL

While established companies aim their big guns at traditional and familiar big targets, there are fast-charging Digital Estate compa-nies that, through guerrilla-type tactics, look to walk into those companies' camps and steal their flags. The new companies are un-bound by brand equity to protect and are not faced with looking at the new markets as secondary, after the primary business. They hire from the ranks of the larger companies, with the promise of re-leasing the creativity and energy of these staffers. They create and launch new products at a lightning pace, using state-of-the-art technology as an integral part of their businesses. These companies promote aggressively and ultimately even attempt to integrate competitors into their service offerings. It's not that the larger com-panies can't act the same way, it's often that there is a lack of *cor-porate will* to do it.

An analogy might be how a company goes about introducing a national account sales program. There is need for total, undying support from the top. Companies find they may have to go through several organizational iterations and several managers before the program works for that company. The process needs to evolve until the process works for the particular company. Interactive strategies at established companies need to go through such a mutation, until everything clicks, with an ultimate comfort with the new media leaders within the organization.

Established companies transforming themselves into interactive leaders can succeed in one of two methods, leadership from the top or leadership from within the ranks. With New York Times Company CEO Lance Primis' support, it was much easier for New York Times Electronic Media President Martin Nisenholtz to rally the troops to create a significant Times' presence online. When support comes from the top, and is strong and consistent, it is possible for the troops to get in line and execute the vision. However, top executives at established companies sometimes grow impatient with lack of short-term results. In approaching the company's Web activities, the mood swing of the top executive oftentimes goes something like this:

Intrigue→Apprehension→Excitement→Euphoria→
Apprehension→Impatience

When leadership is from within the ranks, and mass support within the organization builds to critical mass, the leadership of the company can be coerced into following it, and fund the effort. The challenge then is in continual management of expectations. Champions can come from anywhere within the organization. The most potent force is when leadership, the masses, and the champions all are aligned. Leading companies in the Digital Estate have such a business alignment.

Nowhere in the Digital Estate is the contrast between established and new companies more stark than in the zero-base game. When a large company has a semi-annual sales meeting, some 100 staffers from around the country might be brought in for the gathering. Company management lays out the vision, the staff buys in, and all 100 employees take their marching orders back out to the market. Later that afternoon there's an announcement that negates all that was said. Established companies are expected to stay the course; a quick change makes the company management look erratic. In contrast, when an Internet-based startup company does the same thing, it is *expected* that it will change its strategy by the afternoon. Not only is it expected, it is rewarded! The company is viewed as quick on its feet, nimble to adapt to market change. The market is extremely forgiving of the Internet companies, while holding established companies to different standards.

TABLE 14-1. The View from the Market

	ESTABLISHED COMPANY	DIGITAL ESTATE COMPANY
High revenue results	"Sure, but can they keep it up?"	"This company has great promise."
Change in strategy	"They don't understand the market"	"They're moving with the market."
New product	"How does it affect that other product they have?"	"Great addition to the product line."
Report of layoffs	"Good move on management's part."	NA
High benefit	Reengineering	Engineering
Bugs in product	"They blew it."	"They'll get it right."
Product expectation	"It must be perfect."	"It should be pretty good."
Marketing expectation	Flawless, earth-moving, creative	Clever, creative
Downsizing	Good News	Bad News
Upsizing	Bad News	Good News

When Netscape launched its popular World Wide Web navigator program, it decided to keep launching new versions of the product because it viewed the revisions as more important than launching perfect products. The company made the latest Beta versions available for free on the Net, so consumers could come and get them directly, run them through their paces, report bugs, and allow Netscape to fix the problems in the next version. The company even offered a bounty to people who identified new flaws. When a large, well-established company launches a product, it is expected to be fully tested, bug-free, and ready for mass consumption. This requires the established company to invest more in internal testing processes and increases cycle-time to market. For example, when DEC, IBM, and HP introduce products, it is expected that they will be flawless. In addition, the larger the company, the more difficult the task of communicating and maintaining the vision for all. The smaller companies live in a world of constant change and high speed as part of the equation, so if a particular message isn't immediately communicated to all, it is less of an issue, since everyone's head is down with an intense work-focus, and they generally already understand the company's overall objectives. Those companies don't have as many internal components to line up.

LIFE AT GROUND ZERO

Unicom Publications is the electronic publisher of *Broadband Telephony Buyer's Guide,* which was created to serve to the worldwide telecom, cable, and wireless industries with an online directory for the people who design, operate, or maintain complex transport networks.[1] The guides list thousands of products targeted to buyers in the data, cable, cellular, and telecom industries, and it links to more than 4,000 products from companies that supply equipment to those industries. Among the companies whose brands are included at the *Buyer's Guide* location on the Net are AT&T, Eastman Kodak, American Power Conversion, Cincinnati Bell, Dow Chemical, Sony, Panasonic, Alpha Technology, Siecor, Canoga Perkins, and ADC Telecommunications. Many of the companies also provide additional content for the *Guide's* users.

Unlike many companies that created Web sites that contain lists that simply link to other corporate Web sites, the *Broadband Telephony Buyer's Guide* provides content through descriptions of its listed companies' technologies, products, applications, and specialized service. Users are encouraged to send e-mail inquiries to listed companies and those companies are encouraged to add content to their corporate descriptions to encourage more inquiries.

The company was started in October 1995 in Boca Raton, Florida, by Ellen Caravello, a former Wall Street investment banker in her midfifties, and her husband Ron, a telecommunications engineer in his late sixties. While the pair never considered themselves publishers, they viewed the Net as the most significant phenomenon to impact both commerce and culture since the printing press and the telephone.

The couple decided to focus on creating a unique Net-based service within an industry in which they had both spent many years. They viewed the biggest challenge as finding ways to harness and leverage the move to an internetworked world. After four months of surfing the Net, learning and analyzing, the couple decided that the *Guide* should be more than just an enabling linking service: It had to provide content. Electronic Publisher Ellen Caravello:

> Up until the emergence of the World Wide Web as a commercial platform, suppliers to the telecom, cable, and wireless industries used traditional communication paths to provide information to their constituents: print buyer's guides, magazine advertisements, published articles, direct mail, and a multitude of static application materials. We saw this as the opportunity. Traditional print buyer's guides, while the mainstay of the industry, generally have a one-year shelf life and present no opportunity for updates, in an industry where technology changes daily. And there are many of them within several industries that are converging quickly, and where the roles of supplier and provider are changing. So the challenge was to create a dynamic, real-time resource for the converging industries. Our objective became to help users find additional resources and provide companies with a forum for presenting technologies, products, applications, and services in real-time and online.
>
> The next challenge was how to present the resources online. As we used online resources to find information, we learned more and more about how people use Web search engines and decided to take advantage of these engines by creating individual home pages for each of the categories of the buyer's guide. So if someone was searching for modems, or monitoring systems, or fiber optic cable, the search engines would direct them to our site.
>
> We then created a list of categories. It started with more than 1,000, then we narrowed it down to 400, and now it's up to 700. Then we actually wrote the code for each individual page, because in those days automatic home page programs didn't exist, or no one told us about them! When we went online in mid-October we had created more than 1,000 individual URLs, listing approximately 500 companies and 500 categories.
>
> We chose the first group of companies from each of the three industry segments and published a name, address, phone, fax, and a short description of the company's products or services and assigned them to their related categories. That was the beginning of the content.

Then we added a tag line that provided an e-mail address for additional information, similar to the print media's 'reply cards,' and we started mailing leads out every week. People often didn't provide usable information, they said 'just send product information' and listed their e-mail address, which led us to creating a feedback form with our visitor's name, company, title, address, phone, fax, e-mail, and request. We instantly were delivering qualified leads to companies, in many cases via e-mail. Our most creative e-mail lead came from China. It was a PTT engineer who needed a digital cross connect system and, using the keyboard, he created an entire diagram, on an e-mail, of a digital cross connect system. Another company's chief engineer published a three-page formal equipment request and sent it to 10 of our companies.

We started mailing these requests to companies and asking them all for e-mail addresses to automate the process. We got e-mails and, meanwhile, traffic on the site was increasing, which generated more leads. Companies began evaluating the leads that we were sending, and asked if they could add more content to their pages, so we added more content for them, created a search engine for our site, and automated the delivery of the e-mails, generally to the desk of the sales and marketing department. This was the birth of our lead generation business.

We were then processing more than 2,000 leads a week, were working seven days a week, and had not yet charged anyone for anything! We learned that some of our listed companies were not yet online, some were considering going online and many who were online were not generating as many leads from their own site as they were getting from ours.

At the end of February, an advertising executive saw the site, asked if we were selling advertising, which brought us to the next plateau. We created the *Product Review Guides*, with two-inch square pictures with fifty-word descriptions. This was immediately understood by all marketing people, whether they were online or not, since they were standard in the print advertising world. However, we added the Internet phenomenon of rotating advertising banners and a business was born! We then added button banners and redesigned the site to create 'real estate' to sell.

Meanwhile, a company asked us if we were interested in providing the only online demonstration of a new telecom technology on Broadband, and we said yes, and when they asked if we would do all the press releases, we again said yes, and when they asked if we would invite all of our users to test it out, we said yes.

Then another company that assists companies in doing business with the U.S. Government asked if we could provide a business development site for them and they would make the *U.S. Government's Commerce Business Daily's* database available to our users with a free password so that they could search the database for opportunities related to assisting the government in upgrading its communication infrastructure!

Ron and I see *Broadband* as the usher bringing our industry's professionals to the front door of many of our listed companies' Web sites. To further support this thought, one day we got a call from RELTEC, the Reliance/Comtec Group. A committee had been studying our site for several weeks, as an interim place to position their company prior to going online themselves.

One of our companies asked if we could design their huge corporate site, so we started that process. That led to us working with them to write an operations, maintenance, and management manual that will be provided with a user's license. We will design the site so that their personnel can take over its operation, maintenance, and management over time. We've been approached to place 300 Korean telecom manufacturers online. If there were only enough hours in the day to pursue all this business!

Life at ground zero is expensive both in time and money, and it may be the entrepreneur's dream, only time will tell.

Within six months of launch, the *Broadband Telephony Buyer's Guide* was handling 100,000 requests per week, from almost every country in the world. Whether in Silicon Valley, Silicon Alley, or Boca Raton, leading companies in the Digital Estate realize that they have an opportunity to launch a business from the ground up, challenge previous models, and stake out turf where established companies are unlikely to go. Says Ellen Caravello: "We *are* ground zero."

AGGREGATE ME?
NO, I'LL AGGREGATE YOU!

At ground zero, part of the brand strategy game concerns who does what to whom, and who does it first. Established companies, especially content providers, are able to aggregate their own brands under a common umbrella. This gives those companies a fast start, since their brands are known entities in the physical world. There is a potential downside, in that they tend not to go outside their own brands, and also tend to keep the product lines intact, as individual brands under one roof. While there may be 10,000 companies each doing one thing that they each do well, another company can come along and aggregate it all. The aggregator is immediately in a better market position than the aggregated. For example, when CNET wanted to enter the navigation agent field, rather than launching yet another navigation agent into a market crowded by the likes of Yahoo!, InfoSeek, and AltaVista, it simply aggregated the best-known agents under one roof and called it search.net. The company actually created a new brand comprising the other brands!

AGGREGATING AT GROUND ZERO

When DKS Interactive entered the market, it was because it saw a need for businesses to be able to obtain product information about a broad base of businesses.[2] DKS was established as a new part of Dan Koosh Studios, which started in 1980 in Southern California. The core business dealt with commercial and advertising photography, video production, and graphic design. The interactive group was launched as a full-service multimedia production house specializing in electronic design, multimedia productions, and Internet and intranet communications.

The interactive group created BusinessWorld, a Web site containing product information from thousands of companies from numerous industries, such as agriculture/farming, heavy industries, travel and leisure, transportation, computers and electronics, real estate, and agriculture. In finance, it aggregated companies such as the Bank of America, Chase Manhattan Bank, Hong Kong Bank in New Zealand, Visa, Mastercard, and CyberCash.

It then sold billboard advertising to appear at the top of the listings to CNNfn, the Atlanta-based-company's financial network, investment bankers The Geneva Group, and e.schwab, the online trading investing service. The company saw a need for an online trading center. In its news area, it aggregated such brands as CNN, *The Economist*, CBS Sports, NBC News, and *The Sunday Times*. Because the information could be frequently and easily updated, companies found the idea of online product offerings of high value. Says founder Dan Koosh:

> At the time of our launch, Web sites were very limited on the Internet, Net searchers were just beginning to hear names like Yahoo!, Netscape was just becoming a familiar name, and the advertisers were beginning to explore the possibilities of a new medium called the Internet.
>
> Our main focus was to create and establish an international yet solid platform, a trade center, on the Internet and make it possible for companies, advertisers, or just curious viewers worldwide to be able to find specific business-related information they needed with just a click of their mouse. BusinessWorld became popular on the Web very quickly.
>
> From the very beginning, we have been receiving numerous inquiries to include other Web sites to BusinessWorld, but we chose to be selective about the links we listed on our site. We strongly believe that any Web site that is specialized and has specific information or categories for viewers will do fine on the Internet. By monitoring BusinessWorld viewers on a daily basis and receiving thousands of e-mail messages for the past 12 months, we found it very interesting and impressive to announce that our visitors are becoming more and more professionals, who are seriously seeking information pertaining to their businesses. This is very exciting and also very much rewarding for us, when we find ourselves closer to our original goal, which was to serve professional viewers when we created BusinessWorld in the first place.

The larger or more established companies don't stand to get beaten by one company, they stand to get beaten by thousands of companies. While they set their sights on their traditional, potentially formidable competitors, the new interactive companies are multiplying like rabbits and swarming over the landscape like ants. One at a time, these Lilliputians may not show up on a large company's radar until many of them combine to take a hill. And in the Digital Estate, just about anything, or anyone, can be aggregated.

POTENTIAL AGGREGATED FUTURE PRODUCTS:

- The top 20 business stories each day aggregated from *The Wall Street Journal, BusinessWeek, Forbes,* and *Fortune.* Business readers pay the aggregator for the convenience factor.

- *cans.com.* An aggregator creates a consumer shopping service comprising virtually any canned good, delivered within 24 hours. Products shipped from manufacturer to aggregator fulfillment center. Consumers pay for the service.

- *super-duper-mall.com.* A one-stop shop containing only the largest of the large virtual malls, all under one roof.

- *calling-all-parents.com.* A grouping of all parent chat services, by category.

- *aggregation.com.* The ultimate in aggregation: an aggregation of the aggregators.

WINNING STRATEGIES FOR ESTABLISHED COMPANIES

So what are companies to do in context of Ground Zero in an internetworked world? Established companies need to enter the fray, while maintaining their core business. The newer companies, who won't remain new for long and will face growing pains, and still yet newer competitors, need to maintain their heritage.

- *Partnering.* It is difficult for Internet startup companies to scale, so they often seek partnerships with larger companies with stronger infrastructures. Larger companies can seek opportunities in these partnerships. Caveat: When larger, un-Net-savvy companies hook up with smaller, Internet-oriented companies, they may want to stay at arm's length, and certainly not worry about polished strategies.

- *Spreading out.* Get into several interactive business segments in several different places. Vision can be focused, while execution can include spreading the risk.

- *Being very new.* Some are able to see the world only through their own eyes. When they come to moving to interactive product strategies, they look only in terms of their current product line, or the way they have conducted their traditional business, rather than exploring totally new product areas that could leverage either the market perception of the company or its core competencies. It is common for a company's initial Web presence to simply transfer its corporate brochures onto the Web, rather than to formulate a comprehensive interactive strategy that fully utilizes the medium.

- *Rethinking financials.* Perhaps a company can't make a profit in its historical and traditional methods on the Net. Media companies that traditionally derive revenue from advertising and subscription fees, for example, may collect service fees for new products. Rather than using the World Wide Web as a branding and promotional vehicle, hotels might find they can offload reservations to consumers, saving internal reservation agent fees. Thoroughly thinking through the revenue model, with constant reevaluation, is critical.

- *Communicating.* While established companies often have communications processes in place, it is more challenging to spread the word of how the move to a networked world will affect the particular company, its products, and its people. A clear message needs to get out.

WINNING STRATEGIES FOR SMALLER/NEWER COMPANIES

- *Partnering.* Finding a company with complementary skill sets, such as solid infrastructure, can facilitate scalability. The challenge companies find is mixing the entrepreneurial spirit and work style of a startup with that of an established company. In an ideal world, the large company provides infrastructure, but doesn't smother the smaller partner. Newer companies also have been successful partnering with newer companies, with complementary skill sets. When Internet startup DoubleClick and the Internet Advertising Network combined, they added complementary skill sets, combining a technology-based company with deep technical know-how, with a company well-versed in advertising sales. They ended up with a high-tech advertising service on the Net.

- *Staying Fast.* The successes by the leading companies in the Digital Estate have been partially due to the speed at which they operate, from product conception and launch, through revisions, adaptations, and turn-on-the-dime business models, without short-term pressure for immediate profits. As these companies digest exponential growth, remaining ahead of the market becomes paramount.

- *All Eyes on the Ball.* One of the greatest strengths of the newer Digital Estate companies has been the focus, usually from the top. As more companies and consumers get wired, an increasing number of new opportunities in new markets will face the startups, which may be tempted to move to what looks like more fertile ground. Keeping all eyes on the ball will get tougher.

- *Staying Plugged In.* As companies grow at a feverish pace, keeping the original vision and rapidly evolving tactics communicated to the newcomers will prove to be more difficult. Though technologically advanced and certainly e-mail connected, these fast-paced companies often lack the internal communication processes of more established companies.

Part of the nimbleness of the younger companies is that many of them are run by people who are under 30, and they lack the business experience of their counterparts at more established companies. They are less likely to be conservative about jumping in with both feet, and throwing caution to the wind. Their work habits and focus are intense, they live the Net environment, and they strive for fast and large success.

Leaders of the newer, smaller companies in the Digital Estate consistently say that the established companies, small to large, have an advantage, but almost always fail to recognize and exploit it. Core business revenue prevents companies from viewing Internet business as much more than brand or service extensions of the core business. As the CEO of one Silicon Valley startup company put it: "When I wake up every day, I just pray that the incumbent companies don't become smart enough today to recognize their opportunity. And they don't."

BUMPS ALONG
THE I-WAY

No pain, no gain. It goes with the territory. You've got to walk before you run. The leaders of the Digital Estate have lived these clichés and more. Not everything in the Digital Estate is a bed of roses. Plenty of stories about the hard times that accompany success never get widely reported.

A common misperception is that the Net is a lawless territory, like the romantic notions of the old American West, where the opportunities are vast and navigation is risky. Some imagine bands of blue-jeaned young outlaws, packing keyboards and high-speed modems, who make up their own rules on-the-fly. They will become multimillionaires after widely publicized IPOs, which set market capitalizations grossly out of proportion to established, profitable businesses. All the while, farsighted governments and corporate partners are laying tracks to build a viable infrastructure, waiting for the dust to settle so that law, order, and bureaucracy can again prevail. The vision is colorful, but inaccurate.

The Net is not a territory to be tamed. It is a system that has become decidedly more than the sum of its parts. It is a revolution, a movement. It is not just another medium that can be niched into preestablished demographic formulas. There is an inherent incoherence of the medium, with constant change part of its nature. Because the move to an internetworked environment is filled with the unexpected and the unanticipated, many companies, large and small, have been caught off guard more than once.

TOP **10** REASONS WHY COMPANIES
SHOULD BECOME MEMBERS OF
THE DIGITAL ESTATE

10. They can then dream of being just like the Internet startups, with IPO windfalls and great new market caps.

9. Those ex-biotech investors need a place to go.

8. So they won't be a total embarrassment to their kids.

7. Those who lived through the PC revolution can do it all over again, this time on a network.

6. Just for once, the CEO can go to the board and say: "but we'll be the only company NOT doing it."

5. Their chances will be higher of rubbing shoulders with a twenty-something multi-millionaire, who they can say they knew when.

4. Instead of getting all those free PC magazines and newspapers, they can get all those free Internet magazines and newspapers.

3. They can then surf the Net at the office without feeling guilty.

2. When they read the Digital Estate book, they can say they already were a member.

1. It's better than being known as a member of the analog estate.

The road to a wired world will continue to have plenty of bumps. How, then, does a company incorporate the unexpected into its business model? Here are some companies that have navigated a few of the moguls.

MISTAKE LEARNING

Since commercial development of the Net is still in its infancy, even with its explosive growth, no matter how carefully companies plan, surprises and glitches are inevitable, mainly because there are so few rules or standards to go by.

In addition to unlearning from past practices, Digital Estate leaders experience what I previously described as *mistake learning* or mis-learning, as a way to reevaluate the potential injury or value of a particular mistake. Digital Estate leaders learn how to reevaluate mistakes in the context of what it teaches them about working in the new environment. Without getting "out there" and being kicked around by the dynamics of the Net, companies can't figure how to proceed. Even companies such as *The Wall Street Journal*, which launched a paid subscription, online version of the paper, understood this early on. At launch, the paper acknowledged that it was pioneering a paid, information service, which was contrary in an environment where almost everything was free. Neil Budde, Editor-in-Chief of *The Wall Street Journal's* Interactive Edition says, "We recognize this is the Internet and we have to be flexible. If it doesn't work, we'll try something else."[1]

One of the standard operating procedures for most software developers is the public trial or beta testing of its products. Companies give their product to users willing to test it for free, in exchange for input on flaws and bugs, so that the developers fix them before final release. Much the same holds true for Digital Estate companies who regularly experiment with the launch of new products and services. Something that doesn't work or needs fine tuning is not an indication that the launching company hasn't done its homework or that it is sloppy in its preparation. In the Digital Estate, user feedback is considered essential.

Even the most established companies with decades of business learning under their corporate belts must accept the inherent youthfulness of the new medium. Conducting business in an internetworked world will be qualitatively different, with glitches and full-blown mistakes integral to the process. Mislearning is way of transforming these bumps into unexpected opportunities.

For example, when AT&T made its grand entrance into the Internet business, it did so with great fanfare. At a live, coast-to-coast video press conference, the company announced that it would offer five free hours a month of its WorldNet Internet service to each of its 90 million residential and business phone customers. Allowing for a couple of weeks of hype to spread the news, AT&T launched the service at a party at its New Jersey headquarters in Bridgewater. There were balloons and hot dogs and offers of free software. Who expected more than 5,000 people to appear to grab the free disk offer? Not AT&T, who had pre-produced 5,000 disks for a crowd that exceeded 5,500 customers. Hundreds walked away empty-handed. Similarly, AT&T received almost a quarter of a million requests through its 800 number within days of the announcement, causing a shipping delay of up to six weeks.

The company faced two problems. One was the unexpected response, which led to a second, more serious problem. The company needed to get its service up and running, but it couldn't adequately handle the demand. Within nine weeks of launch, more than 600,000 customers requested access disks, and the company had signed up more than 150,000 customers. Rather than risk losing customer support, AT&T instituted a Quality Inspector Program that awarded customers points for each improvement to the service. The unexpected demand created an opportunity for AT&T to engage its customers in the building of the service. Knowing the likelihood that the system would experience glitches due to overloads helped circumvent frustration for customers, who would not only expect to experience some problems, but who would be rewarded for identifying them.

Some of the numerous examples of the growing pains experienced by companies as they moved into the Net environment include:

- Volvo spent about $100,000 developing and promoting what started out as an electronic brochure. In addition to general information about the company and its cars, the site provided an opportunity for people to send e-mail to Volvo. People would occasionally write things like: "Nice Web site, but the sunroof on my 850 leaks." The problem arose because many state lemon laws require responses to such complaints within a specified time, otherwise the manufacturer has to buy back the car. Since Volvo did not staff the Web site with people qualified to respond to such complaints, it became a tool not to increase sales but to potentially damage them. As a result, the e-mail feature had to be shut down within a few weeks.

- When *The New York Times* launched its online version on the Web, it decided to ask everyone who entered to register, free of charge, so that it could identify who was using the service. What The *Times* didn't count on were an unprecedented 1,000 registrants an hour. The *Times* had to temporarily disconnect the registration system, allowing users to come back without putting in a password, until they could add more computing power.

- IBM experienced a similar overload problem when it staged live Internet coverage of the chess game that pitted a human against a computer: The match was between world chess champion Gary Kasparov and IBM's computer intelligence Deep Blue. Who would have imagined that millions of people would want to view the match online? The company had to double the computing capacity virtually overnight (Kasparov won). IBM experienced a more serious public relations challenge when its highly-publicized technology at the 1996 Olympic Games in Atlanta experienced highly-visible glitches, most notably in the information feeds to news organizations, for use in print, broadcast, and Net distribution.

- America Online made history in August 1996 when a routine maintenance check shut down the popular online service for almost nineteen hours. The plight of the six million plus users, including a significant number who rely on the service to conduct business, made headlines on the nightly news and in newspapers across the country. The public snafu proved to be costly for the company, in image and in credibility. America Online compensated its subscribers with one day of free service, at an estimated cost of about $3 million.

- The Department of Transportation got into the act when it fined Virgin Atlantic $14,000 for posting allegedly misleading advertising, the first time the government had enforced its regulations on the Internet. Virgin Atlantic had posted an advertisement on its Web site for its fare between London and Newark, New Jersey, that failed to include taxes.

- When Hasbro launched its Web site for the popular Action Man, a European version of GI Joe, it loaded its splash page with technically-oriented graphics, which clearly were not appealing to its target audience of 12-year-old boys. When Hasbro realized that forty percent of the visitors to the site never went past the first screen, it revamped it, increasing the number of visitors by fifty percent. Average site time per person increased from eight to eleven minutes.

YOU WANNA TALK ABOUT CHANGE?

Some companies have been forced to make major business turns because of the Net, as its explosive growth and dynamics caught even the most astute observers by surprise.

Prodigy was the first of the major proprietary services to offer a ramp onto the World Wide Web, followed quickly by America Online and CompuServe. The gateways make it possible for subscribers to cruise the Internet while remaining inside the structure of the service. The next step for these services was the move to the Web itself. In addition to being proprietary services and experienced aggregators of content, the Web-based offerings, such as AOL's GNN and CompuServe's Wow!, positioned the services as Internet access providers. Subscribers paid competitive fees for access both to the Internet and to the substantial content gathered under the umbrella of the host service.

The move to the Web may, in retrospect, seem a natural evolution. The Web didn't exist when these services first set up shop.

What is so extraordinary about the case of the online services is the speed at which the companies adapted and implemented systems that seem to compete directly with their core business. The reactions of these companies to the explosion of the Web demonstrate the need to think fast and to remain flexible.

However, the Microsoft Network's (MSN) flash and flicker arrival into the fray drives the point home. The initial plans for MSN positioned the offering as a proprietary service, with a transaction-based revenue model. Microsoft would provide the platform, including technology, payment systems, client and server software, and development tools that would establish MSN as the new standard in online services, in much the same way that AOL's friendly user interface helped it grow.

Content providers would be free to develop their own business models and share the revenues that their content generated. Microsoft bundled MSN into Windows 95, providing an icon to make it easier for buyers of the popular operating system to join the service. The proprietary online services, at the time, considered this an unfair advantage.

Then along came the graphical user interface, the World Wide Web, and Internet usage exploded. Of course, Microsoft and other companies anticipated growth and development of the Internet, but no one really anticipated the magnitude and speed at which the Net would take hold. Microsoft, which had always planned for full Internet access, totally changed course, redefined its online strategy, and reorganized to effect the change. In December 1995, less than six months after MSN was launched, Microsoft announced that it was repositioning MSN as an Internet service using open standards. The company even reached an agreement with longtime rival Sun Microsystems to adapt Java, a cross-platform programming tool, for Windows.

The key to MSN's success and survival rests in Microsoft's ability to keep long-term goals focused, while remaining flexible at the product or project level. "Iteration" is a Microsoft term for the willingness to change in the face of evidence gained by experience. Microsoft was willing to accept that the strategies on which it had built its huge success were not necessarily those that would ensure future success. By accepting the Net as an open-ended medium that cannot be dominated by a single standard, Microsoft opened itself to more opportunities than if it had maintained the proprietary approach of MSN.

Open systems like the Net require open-ended strategies. Prominence, not dominance, is the rule, with reliance on flexibility, agility, and collaboration.

WOES FROM THE FRONT LINES

VCast is a fledgling Silicon Alley company in the online/offline category, targeting the automatic delivery of information from the Web to the desktop. The company struggled to find exactly the right business model on which to launch its business. Here's their tale, from CEO Don Tydeman, who has been leading the search for the right plan.[2]

> I am the CEO of VCast, a tiny startup company housed in one, thirty-foot-square room of an old office building at the corner of Lafayette and Spring streets. There are only three of us officially on staff and only one of us actually draws a meager paycheck. Our burn rate is under $20,000 a month. This includes rent, travel, a T1 Internet connection, my parking fees, and company-sponsored lunch. But we each have a corner office. The problem we face, which is a problem for almost everyone in this business, is the newness of the whole thing. New technology is enabling us to communicate in ways that have never before happened. There's no precedent, no history, no prior learning from which to project. There's no past, there is only the present and the future to work with. Christian Stumm, our founder and technology guru, invented an elegant piece of software code which, when installed on a PC connected to the Internet, will fetch specified information files on the Web without the user having to do a thing. The information installs itself on the user's local drive and is ready to be used. There's a benefit to the user, because valued information arrives automatically without the hassle of finding it on the Web. And there's a benefit to the content provider, because information is regularly accessed.
>
> Now, how do you turn this technology into a business? Having been a print-based publisher for the past 15 years, I could see a tremendous benefit for Web publishers who would rather deliv-

er their online sites, with advertising, rather than wait for a visit. I could also see how a software retailer could deliver entire programs to users overnight. Want multimedia? No problem! Bandwidth is never an issue because delivery of full-motion multimedia takes place when you aren't at the computer, like in the middle of the night. We can deliver movies, commercials, animation, whatever. When you come to your PC in the morning, sit back and enjoy the show.

But how should we best position this technology? Is it a product, a service, a system, or all three? Do we sell it to content providers or do we become a content provider ourselves to maximize the benefit of the technology? Every business book I've ever read says to know what business you're in, but I'm not sure that matters in this environment. Besides, every business book I've ever read was about a world that had nothing to do with this new order. If we license our technology to others will we ever have a real business? Would the inventor of the horseshoe have made more money by applying his invention to horse racing and transportation or in becoming a blacksmith? As has been said, first we shape the tools and then the tools shape us.

This is what marketing on the Web is about for many of us. Even the mightiest of all technology companies, Microsoft, is trying to use its technology to get into other businesses like media, banking, and entertainment. So, what business is Microsoft in? If it doesn't matter to them then why should it matter for us? We debate our course and strategy constantly. Actually, these debates often get quite ugly and personal, but they are an absolute necessity for maintaining sanity. Because we are so small it is easy for us to be reactive to change. We have convinced ourselves that this is an advantage, but it has its drawbacks as well. We have changed our business model so many times that we have come to view it as a living document that is constantly reacting to the latest technology rumors from Redmond, Menlo Park, or Wall Street.

The competition is unrelenting, and there are other companies invading our space. Four months ago we were alone in our category and today we are one of about a dozen. We are analogous to surfers trying to catch a big wave. We see it approaching and begin to ride. But it instantly becomes crowded with others. Should we cut out of this wave and catch the next one, which may be even bigger, or do we hang tough and try to smash into our competitors? Is it possible to use this wave to be better positioned for the next one? Can we do both?

It becomes clear to us that we must be in two worlds at once: the present and the future. We must have a business model which today can create revenue, compete successfully against rivals, and instantly be able to catch the next technology wave. But we need to find the next wave as well. For us that will have to be multimedia. The promise of bandwidth will not be a reality for many years, but it is where everything is going. We have the technology to deliver large video files overnight containing news, movie trailers, and games. This is a very big wave and no one is riding it. Yet! We will be alone on this wave for only two or three months and then it will begin to get crowded. We must acquire the people, marketing, infrastructure, and capital very quickly in order to sustain our lead. This will be a fun ride.

VIRTUAL DISORDER

In the Net environment, disorder is a form of productive chaos, which characterizes the open nature of the Net. Digital commerce is antithetical to brick and mortar. Digital entertainment creates mass customization with users able to create their own programming. Digital reach negates geographic barriers. Disorder, in this sense, is merely the reality of random access. While digitalization certainly creates great opportunities, it can also be disorienting.

First Virtual, one of the major players in the burgeoning field of electronic payment systems, is an extreme example of the opportunities and pitfalls of working inside the Net.[3] The company, as it's name implies, takes virtuality seriously. First Virtual was started as a virtual company, and, although growth required some centralization of its work force, the company still remains largely virtual, in practice and in vision. After the first year of operation, here is what the executives at First Virtual discovered:

> First Virtual attracted notice as an extreme example of a "virtual company." The company was certainly unusual in its initial organization: The four founders lived in San Diego, Orange County, Silicon Valley, and northern New Jersey. We promptly hired ad-

ditional team members in distant parts of the same and other states. There were no physical offices until 15 months after the company was founded (8 months after the system became operational). The servers were set up in a high-security EDS machine room in a suburb of Cleveland; the data 800 number was answered in Atlanta, GA; the voice 800 numbers started out in Portland, Oregon, but were then changed to move around from city to city. Marketing was handled from Washington, D.C., and public relations from San Diego. The company hired lawyers in San Diego, Los Angeles, Chicago, New York, Washington, and Cheyenne. Legally, First Virtual is a Wyoming corporation. This is, to say the least, not a typical corporate organization!

Some aspects of this decentralization worked well, and were quite fun. But there were serious problems as well. While three of the four founders were long-time Internet veterans, one was not, and approximately half of the early employees (all the nontechnical ones) were Internet "newbies" who had to learn the ropes of working with others completely via the Internet. This is a non-trivial endeavor. The larger the company grew, the more seriously its productivity was impeded by communications difficulties, which ultimately led to the decision to consolidate the bulk of operations, and particularly new hires, in a small number of offices.

The biggest problems in running a distributed company were the more mundane aspects of any corporation—administrative tasks, scheduling meetings, making presentations to customers, and so on. It was much harder to gather people together for informal brainstorming sessions and other creative gatherings. The distributed nature of the company made it difficult to ensure that the company would speak with a unified voice in its public statements, and to avoid wasteful duplication of efforts. It is also far harder to integrate new hires into a virtual environment, particularly if they are not by temperament the kind of independent workers who work best in such an environment.

Given these problems, it is tempting to say that "virtual companies don't work." This is an oversimplification, and an irrelevant one in any event. First Virtual, in particular, could not have been created any other way. Its four founders were well-known, extremely successful people who lived in four different parts of the country, and it was never a serious possibility that three of them would relocate in order to start a highly-speculative new venture.

More generally, the fact is that almost any Internet service company will by nature be somewhat "virtual," if only because of the need to support fully international operations. If you're going to be able to communicate with Internet-based customers around the world, in many languages, it is almost inevitable that you will end up with operations spread out to many countries, connected to each other primarily via the Internet. Thus the right question to ask is not "should an Internet company be virtual?" but rather "how virtual should an Internet company be?" or perhaps "how can the advantages of a distributed company be maximized and the disadvantages minimized?"

What worked best in our virtual company were creative projects executed by small, strongly-motivated, highly-skilled teams. The basic technologies in First Virtual were all created by such teams, whose members never shared an office. However, the need for communication and clear task delegation among the team members argued for regular in-person meetings. Two-day monthly staff meetings, scheduled on a totally regular basis for the same days each month, have proven sufficient for such tasks.

Having everybody together at a single site is absolutely not a prerequisite for doing business on the Internet, which should be a relief to anyone contemplating serious international operations. However, a distributed operation carries some very specific pitfalls in terms of communication, efficiency, and motivation, which need to be understood and addressed by management early on.

An interesting note to the First Virtual story, and one of great importance to the company, is the fact that one of the founders is severely handicapped and could never have participated in the venture if it weren't for the freedom created by the virtual design of the company. Telecommuting and virtual work will create opportunities for collaborative working models. The significance of the move into virtual work is the extent to which order and control will shift from the management of people to the management of product. Ironically, the very disorder of a digital environment gives rise to Digital Estate companies with the vision to create order out of chaos.

ANOTHER DAY, ANOTHER OPPORTUNITY

Companies in the Digital Estate will be faced with new and unexpected challenges as the networked environment matures. New technologies will turn today's marvels into tomorrow's antiques. Even so, the inherent disorder of communicating and transacting through networks will continue to energize the medium. The Digital Estate rewards mistakes, cultivates contingency, questions incessantly, and thrives on disorder. The unexpected, although it may cause injury occasionally, is a constant reminder that, in a highly energized environment like the Net, anticipation and curiosity make up the foundation for success.

THE DIGITAL ESTATE RULES OF BUSINESS NETIQUETTE

Netiquette is the accepted term for Net Etiquette, which grew out of the online experiences of the earliest users of the Internet. Business Netiquette, as its name implies, is the standard of behavior that governs the commercial development and usage of the Net by members of the Digital Estate.

The evolving rules of conduct are particularly important in this context because the digital environment of the Net makes it impossible to separate business and consumer "real estate." Virtual town-centers, virtual malls, and intranationally aggregated office parks reside in essentially the same space as personal home pages, educational and research networks, and government and nonprofit organizations. All the hundreds of thousands of home pages on the Web—as well as the staggering list of usenets and newsgroups—filter through the same small screen in front of an individual.

Whether filtered through a PC monitor, TV screen, or information appliance, the Net exists independently of any particular user. The business community must respect that, for all its vast commercial potential, the Net is also a personal place—home, neighborhood, or city—for millions. The Rules of Business Netiquette are an attempt to provide general guidelines for keeping the relationship between consumers and businesses a healthy, happy one.

Another function of the Rules of Business Netiquette is to draw on the considerable experiences of members of the Digital Estate who have been out in the digital field discovering, mainly through trial and error, the brass tacks about working in this very different landscape. While many of the standard rules of business conduct apply, the Net creates circumstances that are unique. Privacy, intellectual property rights, e-mail, Web designs, and interactivity have altered the way companies go about their daily routines.

The Rules of Business Netiquette adhere to a standard that goes beyond the more general netiquette norms governing the online behavior of individual users. The potential that makes the Net such an attractive and fertile area for commercial cultivation carries with it a responsibility. Companies would do well to remember that, on the Net, the individual user is always in control and always has choices.

The following Rules of Business Netiquette have been organized into three categories that include the Web, e-mail, and general business principles. In keeping with the collaborative nature of the Net, these rules represent the input of many people who have developed their own standards of business conduct on the Net based on experience.

THE 100 RULES OF BUSINESS NETIQUETTE

1. Be sensitive to customers with older systems. Offer a text-only option for viewing your site on the splash page.

2. Remember that your customers are paying to be online. Provide fast and easy access to your information and content. Don't abuse their time.

3. Organize material logically from the customer's point of view. Ideally, the splash page will be the main page on a site. Be sure to include clear directions for navigating the site on the main page.

4. Keep in mind that the main page of a site serves a variety of functions. It is a map, a front door, and a marketing message all in one.

5. Use the splash page to set the tone and personality of the site, but do so selectively. The tone of the Web site should correlate with the personality of the company.

6. If appropriate, include a time and date stamp. It helps to keep the site current.

7. Use Last Modified dates and traffic counters only if you want your customers to know when you last modified your site or how many visitors you have had.

8. When using icons, particularly those embedded in a graphic design, make sure that they are easy to see and that their function is obvious. Test the design on ten to twenty users to make sure your customers will understand.

9. Include text versions of all icon links.

10. Avoid offending new users to the Net by using heavily-laced jargon or by adopting a "hipper-than-thou" attitude.

11. Do not use bells and whistles just because you can. As bandwidth increases, this issue will become less relevant. Until then, heavy use of graphics, video, and audio programs is time-consuming for the user.

12. Disclose compatibility information, such as, "This page is best viewed by Netscape 3.0 and above."

13. Be sure to include links to the software necessary for a full appreciation of your site. If you say your site uses RealAudio, then make sure it links to a download for RealAudio.

14. Avoid useless pages that serve no purpose. If a page doesn't show or tell the user something, or provide a service, then your site doesn't need it.

15. Include an e-mail address link where appropriate.

16. Include a "Return Home" link on every page.

17. Remember the three-click rule and organize sites logically. The three-click rule states that users will not stay onsite if it takes more than three clicks to access the information they need.

18. Include a FAQ page and an "About the Company" profile on your site. Links to this information should be clearly marked on the main page.

19. Make sure the profile contains all relevant information about the company including snail mail address, telephone and fax numbers, and the appropriate contact with title.

20. If your site sponsors real-time chats, have a system for monitoring the chats. This gives the user a sense of security, and it gives you control.

21. If you use bulletin board postings, be sure to keep them updated and interesting. Design topics appropriate to your community, which will foster conversation.

22. If appropriate to your site, use current events to spice up chats and bulletin board discussions. It is the responsibility of the host, not the visitor, to initiate interactive communication.

23. Anticipate the needs of your users. If your site has databases, provide a search engine on site.

24. Annotating lists is a valuable and time-saving service you can offer your customers. The more useful information you can provide, the better the quality of your site.

25. Keep all links live and test periodically.

26. If you are using your site to launch-and-learn your product make sure that you have a product. Users do not expect perfection in beta products, but they do expect the product to be almost fully functional.

27. Use a logical URL.

28. Register with every possible source of traffic. Search engines are the primary pathways to your corporate front door.

29. Run test searches to make sure your site comes up with each of the search engines.

30. Think through keywords clearly. Imagine how a customer would look for your service or product if they didn't know your company or Web site name.

31. Shield your site if it is still under construction. Only go live after thoroughly testing with real users.

32. Give the user a reason to stay. Use contests, trivia, and other such promotional tactics to draw a user in. If they have come

to access a service, provide it up front. Do not make your customers wade through pages of information, if they have come to use your calculator.

33. Reward users for giving up valuable marketing information. For example, offer a company tee shirt for completing a profile.

34. Systemize your response to e-mail requests. An immediate response stating that the message has been received assures users that you are on the ball. Also, give the user an indication of how long it will be before they can expect a response.

35. Subtle reminders are unobtrusive. Suggest that a user, "Add this page to your bookmarks."

36. Encourage other sites, including noncommercial sites, to link to your site. Personal home pages are an often overlooked resource for directing traffic to a corporate site.

37. Use logical resources, such as PR Newswire and Business-Wire to make appropriate announcements.

38. Do not announce the launch of a "New Site" if what's new is only an addition to an existing site.

39. If you refer to sources of information within your site, then provide hyperlinks to the appropriate site.

40. When linking to another site, link directly to the appropriate page rather than to the home page URL.

41. Ask permission for linking to a site. Unexpected traffic surges created by links can shut a server down.

42. Make sure that you have the appropriate resources to handle the traffic generated by the site. This specifically applies to e-mail. E-mail is your customer service representative on the Web.

43. Think globally. Remember that users from other countries can easily access your site. If you want to tap into international markets, respect their culture and keep in mind that they may not be familiar with idiomatic expressions or respond to pro-American ad campaigns.

44. When advertising, avoid misleading links. If you have a banner for a giveaway, then a click on the banner should take the user straight to the giveaway page.

45. Include the full URL so that people know the address of the resource from a paper copy of your page.

46. Include your URL in all promotional material, such as magazine advertisements, brochures, radio, television, and billboard advertisements.

47. Clearly state the copyright policy for the information and graphics available through your site.

48. Do not simply abandon a site. If you move or close or change names, alert users via e-mail and register changes with appropriate venues, such as search engines.

49. Do not mix personal and business sites. Don't include pictures of the kids unless they are somehow relevant to the business. That's what personal home pages are for.

50. Never post unsolicited mail. Sending ads to newsgroups or mass e-mailings is called spamming. It is an offensive invasion of privacy and will result in a Net response known as flaming. Flames are angry or gibberish e-mail replies sent en masse to a spammer. Flaming wars can shut down a system.

51. When it comes to e-mail, never put anything in an e-mail that you wouldn't want to see on the nightly news.

52. Establish either separate accounts or separate aliases for personal and business correspondence.

53. Have business cards printed with e-mail and URL addresses. The days of hand-scribbled addresses on the backs of cards are over.

54. Think logically when establishing accounts. E-mail systems can be set up so that aliases make sense, such as sales@company.com rather than name@company.com. (While this is technically a function of the system administrator, it doesn't hurt to know the options for your company.)

55. Avoid clever aliases. Use your online name to clearly identify yourself.

56. Learn your e-mail system protocols, such as file attachments, message length limits, filing cabinet options, etc.

57. If using e-mail to contact sources for marketing research, be sure to identify yourself and obtain permission.

58. Follow chain of command procedures. Don't e-mail a CEO unless you have established prior contact.

59. Keep internal e-mail below 50 percent, and external e-mail over 50 percent, if you want to be connected to your market.

60. Be professional and careful about what you say about others in electronic communications. Mail is easily forwarded.

61. Do not use e-mail for sensitive communications.

62. Know and adhere to company e-mail policies.

63. Use a separate alias for newsgroups and usegroup lists. This will keep your business address free of unnecessary clutter.

64. Do not use buddy systems, or electronic alerts that tell a user when another user is online, unless you have been given permission to do so. It is an invasion of privacy.

65. Use Instant Message facilities appropriately. The telephone is a better vehicle for involved conservation.

66. Notify appropriate e-mail correspondents if you will be out of e-mail reach for an extended period of time.

67. Run virus scans frequently, and be sure to alert recent correspondents if you detect a virus on your system.

68. Limit e-mails to one topic per message.

69. Begin your message with an appropriate address (e.g., Linda or Mrs. McGregor), and always include your name at the end.

70. Keep paragraphs and messages short and to the point.

71. Use bullets or asterisks to break up complicated messages.

72. Keep your e-mail clean. Use correct grammar and check spelling.

73. Be sure to proofread a message before sending it out, not only to check for errors, but also to make sure that the content is clear.

74. Use standard casing. UPPER case looks like you are shouting.

75. Acronyms can be used to abbreviate when possible, but messages that are filled with acronyms can be confusing and annoying to the reader.

76. Always identify yourself and your affiliation in e-mail and newsgroup postings. Anonymous online participation is only appropriate in certain chat areas.

77. Use an electronic signature that is no longer than four lines. Otherwise be sure to end correspondence with an appropriate identification such as name, title, and e-mail return address.

78. Use the subject heading to reflect the content of the message.

79. Forwarded messages should also be copied to the original message sender.

80. Tell recipients up front if a message should not be forwarded to a third party, but do not assume that no one else will ever see the message.

81. Do not change the wording in a forwarded message. Do not correct the spelling or the grammar. Remember, it's not your name on the header, but that of the original sender.

82. Read through all subject headings before opening a batch of mail. Frequently, senders will send a second message that cancels out the first.

83. Make sure that the message to which you are responding was sent to you for a response. It may been forwarded as an FYI, or you may have been copied as a courtesy.

84. When sending a long message, indicate it in the subject header by typing in "Long." A message over 100 lines is considered long.

85. Notify a recipient if you are sending important or timely correspondence.

86. When replying to a message, summarize enough of the original sender's message so that your response will have context.

87. Never respond to e-mail messages with one or two words, like "That's good."

88. When you receive an e-mail that requires a response, either respond immediately, or let the sender know when you will.

89. Don't send "thank you" messages in response to information sent to you.

90. Keep your inbox tidy so that it contains only those messages that you still have to take action on.

91. Listen to your customers and respond. Often they will tell you exactly what product or service they would like to buy from you.

92. Listen to the 24-year-olds. Frequently those who are most in tune with the Digital Estate environment are not necessarily those who hold the highest offices. A brilliant idea might be hatched in the mailroom.

93. The Net is a collaborative environment. Reconsider strategies to work with or link to competitors.

94. Use the Net. You don't have to be a surfer to regularly use the Net. Engagement will keep you informed and alert you to trends and problems.

95. Constantly question your business assumptions. Form a habit of asking, "How can we do X online?"

96. Encourage full company participation. Educate your staff, making sure they are familiar with your Web site, both in function and design.

97. Remember that not everyone understands the impact or value of the Net as you do. Use creative demonstrations to help them see the light.

98. Avoid the jargon jungle. Express your ideas in clear, precise language.

99. Participate in discussion groups on- and offline. Brainstorming and feedback are the lifeblood of the Digital Estate. Sharing perspective facilitates healthy growth.

100. Give something back. Provide a useful product or service that enhances the online experience. Businesses in the Digital Estate are active participants in building their environment.

Rules of conduct are never written in stone. They grow and evolve with the world they are meant to order. But the general principles underlying the Rules of Business Netiquette will remain the same. In a digital world, interactivity is paramount. For the Digital Estate, this means keeping the channels of communication open.

The following is a pocket list of the top ten rules for success in the Digital Estate.

TOP TEN RULES OF BUSINESS NETIQUETTE

1. Never put anything in an e-mail that you wouldn't want to see on the nightly news.

2. Do not post unsolicited mail.

3. Remember that your customers are paying to be online. Don't abuse their time.

4. Listen to your customers and respond.

5. Encourage interactivity on your company site

6. Keep internal e-mail below 50 percent, and external e-mail over 50 percent.

7. Remember the three-click rule and organize sites logically. The three-click rule states that users will not stay onsite if it takes more than three clicks to access the information they need.

8. Avoid the jargon jungle. Express your ideas in clear, precise language.

9. Provide fast and easy access to information and content. Don't abuse your customers' time.

10. Give something back to the Net environment. You are the Net.

CHAPTER
SEVENTEEN

WHAT GOES WITH THE TERRITORY

Many issues will not be resolved overnight, even in Net Time. What is the role of the large, established company in the Digital Estate? Where will the Internet startups finish? What does a company have to do today to be a leader tomorrow? Will Netscape be the next Microsoft? What responsibilities, beyond those to shareholders and owners, go with being a member of the Digital Estate? Many companies have already demonstrated strong vision and leadership, social responsibility, and a high respect for the privacy rights of individuals. What is the digital landscape going to look like in a interactive, internetworked world?

THE WAY THE WIND IS BLOWING

No one can be certain of any predictions in this marketplace. Some trends and directions, however, will cause the rapid movement to an internetworked world to continue, drawing more and more people, and more and more businesses, online.

THE SHRINKING GLOBE

The Net is the first truly global, information-based, interactive medium in history. The world has never had the capability to link people globally around common sets of information, with the potential of instantaneous exchange. People can find others with similar interests

THE DIGITAL ESTATE

BUILDING BLOCKS

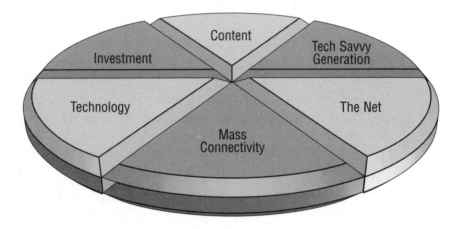

FIGURE 17-1

anywhere on the planet through the Net. Important messages can be made available simultaneously, globally, without filters.

The recommendations to the European Council Europe and the Global Information Society report represents the advice that is being offered all over the globe. It states:

> Why the urgency? Because competitive suppliers of networks and services from outside Europe are increasingly active in our markets. They are convinced, as we must be, that if Europe arrives late our suppliers of technologies and services will lack the commercial muscle to win a share of the enormous global opportunities which lie ahead. Our companies will migrate to more attractive locations to do business. Our export markets will evaporate. We have to prove them wrong. The tide waits for no man and this is a revolutionary tide, sweeping through economic and social life. We must press on.

Governments everywhere are committing resources to build a viable infrastructure for the revolutionary tide, and government and business partnerships are expediting it. The infrastructure will allow a mass infusion of global participants.

- The Peruvian Scientific Network (RPC) provides public access not only to the Internet but also to a bank of computers and classes on how to navigate the network. RPC started in 1991 with $7000 in seed money from the United Nations Development Fund and 40 subscribers. In 1996 the network carried 22,000 subscribers and $4 million in equipment, with expectations of 60,000 subscribers in 1997. The network, which was the first provider of Internet service in Peru, is financed by its members, including universities, hospitals, nongovernmental organizations, associations, and private citizens. All profits are reinvested into maintaining and expanding the network.

- In response to a plan formulated by the Singapore government, the National Computer Board instituted a program called IT2000—A Vision of an Intelligent Island, a 15-year plan to build a communications infrastructure. IT2000 has set its goals on interconnecting computers in virtually every home, office, school, and factory. At the heart of the program is a commitment to the idea that the computer will evolve into an information appliance, combining the functions of the telephone, computer, TV, and more, providing a wide range of communication means and access to services.

- India Online, a joint venture with India's Department of Electronics, Modern Technologies Corp., and Dow Jones subsidiary Datalytics Inc., represents the country's efforts to expand Internet growth. The new company, which will function as an Internet service provider, hopes to capture a market share of 30 percent in the first year of operation. India is also beefing up its IT industry with the addition of another IT park.

- During the last three months of 1995 and the first three months of 1996, 31 countries joined the Internet for the first time, and growth of the network exceeded 100 percent in 60 countries.[1]

AN INCREASE IN THE USE OF DIGITAL MONEY

When consumers become more familiar and comfortable with purchasing online, electronic commerce will explode, dramatically increasing the use of digital money for small and large purchases. The major banking and financial institutions, payment delivery technology providers, financial software services, credit card, micropayment, and smart card companies have formed alliances to break through the security barrier. Companies are working hard to convince consumers to engage in online transactions. Time and convenience will become even more important drivers of Net usage.

- AT&T offers 100 percent protection for WorldNet users who make online purchases with their AT&T Universal credit card, to soothe consumers' fears of making purchases online.

- Lombard Institutional Brokerage in San Francisco generated 10 percent of its sales from Net-based trading. By 1999, CEO Eric Roach hopes to push that to 40 percent.

- By the year 2000, there will be about 3.8 billion smart cards in use. Trials are underway globally.[2]

- The global electronic commerce market will increase to $775 billion by 2000, with micropayments accounting for $7 billion.[3]

THE GROWTH OF INTRANETS

The growth of intranets should increase consumer online participation by introducing a large segment of the population to the Net environment. As intranets familiarize workers with the graphical interface and search methods of the Web, and intranets that are linked into the Internet provide the broad range of online activities and interactivity, workers will also become accustomed to getting information and services when, where, and how they want them.

- Netscape counts 50 percent of Fortune 500 companies among its clients and estimates that a full 70 percent of revenues came from intranet businesses in 1995, when intranets started to take off.[4]

- By the end of 1995, 22 percent of America's 1,000 largest companies were using intranets, and by the close of the second year in the life of intranets, the market should reach $4 billion.[5]

- Seventy-five percent of Fortune 1,000 companies expect to link their intranets to the Internet.[6]

INCLUSION OF THE MAINSTREAM

As the Web and the consumer online services continue to expand into the mass market, the demographics of online users should begin to approach U.S. overall population demographics. The early profile of the Web/online user is a white male, 35 to 40 years old, married with children, and a household income of more than $50,000. The profile should begin to reflect the growing presence of women, children, and seniors online. Some projections include:

- Women will account for 40 percent of online users by the year 2000. Their increased presence represents an important trend as online environments move into the cultural mainstream.[7]

- Of the over-55 demographic, 30 percent own computers, up from 21 percent in 1994. Of those, 25 percent are female. Of the computer owners, 17 percent regularly use online services, with 65 percent of online users having accessed the Internet in the past month.[8]

- By the year 2000, the number of children with access to the Web will reach hundreds of millions.[9]

MEET THE I-GENERS

In addition to the thousands of people and companies who comprise the Digital Estate, more than 30 million, on their way to a billion, people make up the Interactive Generation.[10] These men and women adhere to no uniform political view, work in all occupa-

tions, and are all ages and dispositions. The Interactive Generation, or I-Geners, speak many languages, live all over the world,
and believe in different values. They have no books or music or art
in common. They don't even dress alike.

What I-Geners share, however, is a firm conviction that the future, in terms of living in a networked world, isn't something waiting around the millennial bend. It is happening now. The Interactive Generation comprises individuals who have crossed a
paradigmatic divide into a world unencumbered by the physical attributes of time and space. They understand that, even in its infancy, this new world is already a fundamentally different place because it is changing how humans communicate. The development
of external forms of communication, from cave drawings to hypertext, is a distinguishing characteristic of the species. The I-Gener
is not only willing, but eager to explore the interactive possibilities
created by the Net.

THEY ARE THE NETWORK

The Interactive Generation uses technology comfortably but sees
beyond its limits, expects a certain amount of control over its environment, has a high degree of interest in interacting, has certain
expectations when going online, is forgiving but demanding in its
expectations, and feels like part of the Net. They are the pioneers
who are nurturing and developing a landscape that will one day be
taken for granted. The emergence of the Interactive Generation
opens up a different kind of generation gap.

Couch potatoes were probably never as truly passive as pundits
feared. The advent of channel surfing suggests not a mindless boob
in front of the tube, but a frustrated viewer restless from lack of
participation. What separates I-Geners is their ability to grasp the
potential of interactive appliances and their aggressive desire for
direct control. The I-Geners are unified by a sense of potential for
the future.

Not every I-Gener envisions the same picture of the future,
and not all of the pictures they envision are all positive. Their expectations and their personalities are as varied as their numbers.
But the glue that holds them together as a group is their certainty

that they stand on the threshold of a future irrevocably defined by global, interactive, networks of communication and commerce. Another factor that sets this Generation apart is that it has a built-in shelf life. They know it will not be long before interactivity is taken for granted and that memories of pre-internetworking will be tantamount to recalling the days before machines could fly. After critical mass, everyone will already belong. It is the mission of this first generation to pave the way by becoming the link that connects the world before mass connectivity to the world after its advent.

I-Geners are not blue sky visionaries. They have seen the future only because the future is already out there, in homes, in businesses, in schools, and in the marketplace. What the I-Gener knows is that it doesn't require a special password, a sizable research budget, or even the latest technotoy to see the potential of hundreds of millions of people communicating and interacting on a daily basis. It takes rather a certain amount of daring to stake a claim in a revolution whose only outcome is dramatic change. For the I-Gener, there is simply no choice.

What the Interactive Generation of the Digital Estate understands is that the Net is not a separate environment that individuals can choose or not choose to utilize. In an internetworked world, networks will be the backbone of social and economic life. Just as governments help organize society, and just as cities help organize the daily activities of individuals, networks will increasingly become the primary tool for organizing information. The choice not to participate automatically removes these groups or individuals from the mainstream. This is a generation united under the banner of interactivity, which thrives on making connections. This group of online, interactive, digital individuals are the consumers in the Digital Estate.

THE EVOLUTION OF NEW TECHNOLOGIES

The easier it is to get around in cyberspace, the more people will become comfortable with the environment, and the more technology will make it easier and more rewarding for people to go online. Nowhere has technological development been so rapid as on the Net, since never before has so much processing power been in the hands of so many. The technological ideas and brainstorming continue from Silicon Valley and Silicon Alley, with technology and content continuing to blend. It is this combination of technology and content blended with a technologically savvy generation, large investments, the move to the wired masses, and the Net that combine to form the basis for the future, internetworked world (see Fig. 17-1).

Intelligent search agent technology will evolve to empower individuals to communicate with people and businesses that they want to reach, gather information most relevant to them at the moment of highest value, and make them more productive in their lives. With smart card technology, individuals' profiles can move with them. With network access from virtually anywhere, people will be able to tap into the Net to check schedules, make appointments, purchase products, and conduct business around the globe. Cable modems, increased bandwidth, and information appliances that reside on the network should help bring usage to the masses. The network computer will always be on and ready, like the telephone or cable TV. Being technologically connected will help increase a sense of community. Technologies will continue to enhance the digital environment with elements that facilitate increased levels of interactivity. Researchers such as the Media Lab at MIT will continue to work on defining the future of interaction between humans and machines.

EDUCATION FOR AN INTERNETWORKED WORLD

The Interactive Generation today is only a prototype of what's to come. Interactive education is the most important factor in creating the critical mass to establish the Digital Estate as the center of commercial enterprises. Almost every major company has contributed heavily to various aspects of interactive education. Long-distance learning at the corporate level saves time and money, and it is vastly more efficient and productive because it is continuous.

However, it is the aggressive attempt to bring grammar and secondary schools online that could have the greatest impact. School children growing up in a wired world will take it for granted. Interactivity qualitatively changes the nature of education. Although learning in its purest form has always been to some degree interactive—humans learn first through sensual interaction, then through associative interaction—learning in a networked world changes the dynamics entirely. Teachers will become tutors rather than guardians of adult knowledge. Students will learn through virtual experiences rather than static memorization. Many initiatives are underway to accelerate the pace of interactive education. Education will continue throughout life, with increasing amounts of knowledge available through the network.

- Half of all U.S. public schools have some access to the Internet, up from 35 percent in 1994. To foster the growth of online education, the government allocated $2 billion over five years to help connect every school to the Internet by the year 2000.

- In one of the nation's most ambitious private/public campaigns to provide school children with home computers, Indiana spent $12 million in state funds since 1990 for a program that furnishes home computers, printers, and modems for fourth, fifth, and sixth graders. The program, called the Buddy System, started with grants from Ameritech and the Lily Foundation and involves 7,000 families in 69 elementary schools in 28 Indiana school districts.

- CyberEd, a White House initiative in partnership with nonprofit Tech Corps, provides free hardware, connectivity, training, and Internet access.

- IBM K-12 Education released SchoolVista 2.0. This massive integrated school courseware and management system allows educators to access numerous software packages that schools can tailor to meet their specific needs.

- AT&T's Learning Program Network, a five-year, $150-million program, aims to connect every U.S. public and private elementary school to the Internet. The company also invested $1 million into long-distance learning projects being conducted at 60 universities in 26 countries.

- CyberSurfari '96 Virtual Classroom features lesson ideas for teachers and students. Virtual Classroom will focus on a different theme each month, such as the Olympics, museums of the world, space exploration, national parks, landmarks and international areas of interest, inventions, Rock the Vote, civics and politics, and the Cybersurfari Contest. In the first year, more than 200 schools and 5000 individuals participated.

- Ameritech put up $2 million, in partnership with the U.S. Library of Congress, to bring more American history online. The money will be used to fund a national competition for libraries to digitize parts of their collections. The goal is to make nearly five million items and documents available online by 2000.

LISTENING TO THE WIND

Each of these trends represents a different version of the same story. The Digital Estate may be young, but it is here to stay. The I-Geners of today may pale by comparison to what is coming, but it is they who are the builders of the bridge that will connect today to tomorrow. They are both the market and the market makers of the Digital Estate. The messages from the Valley to the Alley are consistent. You can read between the lines of a few:

- Candice Carpenter, CEO, iVillage: "The big companies are not used to being talked to by an audience. In this environment, the product doesn't live until you have an audience talking back to you. I'm shocked when I see the large companies are standing on the sidelines hoping to jump in later."[11]
- Nick Grouf, CEO, Agents, inc: "The big companies need to catch up if this is all going to happen. The process of filtering to the top of a large company a year ago was that a 23-year-old was the head of an interactive group. He reported to the man who reported to the man who reported to the man who reported to the man who reported to the man who sits next to the head of marketing. As it became more important, that person catapulted to near the top. The sooner these companies can respond effectively, the better it will be, but it's a slow process. A lot of the payback is tough to quantify. This is very much about positioning. The early movers are solidifying their positions. Those who

don't play are going to suffer the consequences. You'll download an album to your house. You can technically download an album now, but there's a channel conflict. But in that channel, there's a lot of expense involved, with shipping, packing, racks. It's frightening to a lot of people."[12]

- Jordan Graham, President and CEO, Electric Classifieds: "The playing field is level. This is the new frontier."[13]

The publicly accessible Web doubles every 53 days.[14] The Internet existed prior to the invention of the World Wide Web, but the Web powered the transformation of the Net into a viable commercial medium, giving rise to the Digital Estate.

Each year brings about a new generation of ideas and standards. Many of the members of the Digital Estate have only grown up with the Web, and some have a distinctly generational view of the technology. Many business lessons have to be learned from them, and some smart companies have incorporated many of these 24-year-olds in their Internet business strategy, planning, and development teams. They are learning.

In less than two years, the static, one-page home page evolved into truly interactive experiences, textured by real-time audio, video, and early three-dimensional, virtual worlds. At the center of this creative commercial storm are the Digital Estate companies, which are dedicated to the potential of a digital environment and which push the Net in every direction. Those companies are committed to the transformations wrought by a shift to a digital economy. Commercialization of the Web is only the first step. Growth will continue and the Digital Estate companies will lead the way in finding new commercial opportunities.

The difference between leaders of the Digital Estate and those who don't get it is not a matter of age or taste. It is more like speaking different languages without a translator. This is precisely the position of the Digital Estate today. In the Digital Estate, the significance of the Net is an either/or proposition: Either one gets it or one doesn't. What is at stake, however, is far more than a matter of perspective. It can make the difference between thriving— and surviving—in an internetworked world.

The stakes are high and they don't just affect businesses. They also are personal, and will affect our children and touch everyone's life. All companies need to participate and to contribute, since the Net is a community. It provides an unprecedented opportunity to redefine the world, change how people communicate with one another and how business is conducted in new, borderless ways, and close economic gaps.

But it will take commitment of the established companies, commitment like that of the leading companies of the Digital Estate. They are helping shape where the world is going. They need more company.

THE VIRTUAL CHAPTER

The Digital Estate will continue to evolve, as more companies and people get wired in. Since a printed book cannot be updated practically, we will use the Web to provide the latest information and business trends as they relate to the Digital Estate.

This regular information stream will reside at the publisher's Web site, at http://www.mcgraw-hill.com/digitalestate.

The site contains the hot-linked version of all the Web addresses of the companies mentioned in the book (see Web Index, page 227), and also will contain regularly updated and related information concerning the Digital Estate.

We view it as a continuous prologue. Readers can contact me directly via e-mail at the site, and online comments and discussion are welcomed.

ENDNOTES

Author's Note: The commercial development of the World Wide Web has been a boon for researchers. Considered standard now, most company sites include an "About the Company" section with history and relevant dates, events, and biographies. Company press releases are also provided onsite. Appropriately, much of the original research for this book derives from material obtained from the Net. The URL Index contains a comprehensive listing of all company sites mentioned in the book. Notation to information gathered onsite is, therefore, excluded from the Endnotes.

CHAPTER 1. THE BIRTH OF THE DIGITAL ESTATE

1. For a detailed look at the growth of the publishing industry in the wake of the French Revolution, see Roger Chartier, *The Cultural Origins of the French Revolution*, trans. by Lydia G. Cochrane, Duke University Press, 1991.

CHAPTER 2. LIVING OUTSIDE THE BOX

1. The following discussion of I/PRO is based on the author's interview with Ariel Poler.
2. The following discussion of Site Specific is based on the author's interview with Seth Goldstein.
3. As reported in NetGuide, March 1996, p. 151.
4. Quote based on conversations with the author.
5. Quote based on conversations with the author.

CHAPTER 3. THINKING SMALL IN THE DIGITAL ESTATE

1. Survey conducted by Roper Starch Worldwide for Canon Computer Systems.
2. According to NetGuide Now!, the vast majority of lists that subscribers sent in contained some, if not, all, of these popular sites.
3. Don Tapscott, *The Digital Economy: Promise and Peril in the Age of Networked Intelligence*, McGraw-Hill, 1996. See pages 51-54.
4. As reported in *Convergence*, March 1996, 15-19.

CHAPTER 4. COMMUNITY RULES

1. The author was Editorial Director at the *Medical Tribune* in the early nineties.
2. The following discussion of iVillage is based on the author's interview with Candice Carpenter and Tina Sharkey-Nederlander.
3. The following discussion of Electronic Classifieds is based on the author's interviews with Jordon Graham.
4. Projections based on research by The Alliance for Converging Technologies
5. Quotes based on conversations with the author.
6. The author was the founding publisher of *Interactive Age*.

CHAPTER 5. AGGREGATING THE WORLD

1. Projections based on research by The Alliance for Converging Technologies.
2. The following is based on the author's visit to the offices of *Asashi Shimbun* and an interview with Mitsuo Deguchi.

CHAPTER 7. NET BONDING

1. The following discussion of Firefly is based on the author's interview with Nick Grouf.

CHAPTER 8. DO THAT VISION THING

1. Survey conducted by KMPG Peat Marwick's Information, Communications and Entertainment and *Upside Magazine*.
2. The following discussion of CNET is based on the author's interview with Halsey Minor.
3. The following discussion of Oracle is based on the author's interview with Laurent Pacalin.
4. As quoted in *Red Herring*, January 1996, p. 24.
5. Ibid.
6. Starwave Case Study, The Alliance for Converging Technologies.

CHAPTER 9. THE BATTLE OF THE BRANDS

1. The following discussion of *The New York Times* is based on the author's interviews with Lance Premise.

CHAPTER 10. TARGETING THE MASSES, ONE AT TIME

1. Advertisement in *AdWeek*, April 1, 1996.
2. The following discussion of DoubleClick is based on the author's interviews with Kevin O'Connor.

CHAPTER 11. THE RADICAL SHIFT IN POWER

1. As reported in *Daily Spectrum: Interactive Media and Online Developer News*, October 20, 1995.
2. A complete copy of the Hewlett-Packard Intranet Case Study can be found at http://www.hp.com:80/AccessGuide/Search.http.

CHAPTER 13. LIVING INSIDE THE NET

1. Survey information is available at http://www.hyperion.co.uk/????

CHAPTER 14. COMPETING AT GROUND ZERO

1. The following discussion of Unicom Publications is based on the author's interviews with Ellen Caravello.
2. The following discussion of DKS Interactive is based on the author's interviews with Dan Koosh.

CHAPTER 15. BUMPS ALONG THE I-WAY

1. As quoted in *The New York Times,* April 29, 1996.
2. The following discussion of VCast is based on the author's interviews with Don Tydeman.
3. A complete copy of "Perils and Pitfalls of Practical Internet Commerce: A Comprehensive View of First Virtual's First Year" is available at http://www.fv.com/company/index.htm??perils.

CHAPTER 17. WHAT GOES WITH THE TERRITORY

1. Internet Domain Survey information can be found at http://www.nw.com/zone/www/top.html..
2. As reported in New Delivery Channels for Banking Services by Killen & Associates.
3. Ibid.
4. As reported in *Convergence*, March 1996, pp. 15-19,
5. Ibid.
6. Ibid.
7. According to Jupiter Communications, Women Online 1996 Report.
8. Based on a study conducted by Intel and Seniornet.
9. According to Jupiter Communications, Kids Online 1996 Report.
10. Based on research by The Alliance for Converging Technologies.
11. Based on author's interviews with Candice Carpenter.
12. Based on author's interviews with Nick Grouf.
13. Based on author's interviews with Gordon Graham.
14. As reported in *Convergence*, March 1996, p. 19.

INDEX

WEBINDEX

CNET	www.cnet.com
Cadillac	www.cadillac.com
CampingNet	www.campingnet.com
CBS	www.cbs.com
Central Europe Online Navigator	www.ceo.cz/ceohome.html
Chicago Online	www.chircords.com
China Internet Corp.	china.com
Christian Science Monitor	www.csmoniter.com
Citibank	www.citibank.com
Coca Cola	www.cokacola.com
CommerceNet	www.commercenet.com
Compucard	www.cuc.com
Conde Nast	www.condenet.com
Court TV	www.courttv.comAOL—go: court
CRAYON	crayon.net
CyberCash	www.cybercash.com
CyberEd	www.whitehouse.gov/wh/eop/ovp/html/.html
CyberHomes	www.cyberhomes.com
CyberSurfari	www.spa.org/cybersurfari/
D.E. Shaw & Co.	sourcedata.com
DataMatters	www.datamatters.co.uk
Department of Transportation	www.dot.gov
DigiCash	www.digicash.com
Digital Equipment Corp.	www.digital.com
Disclosure, Inc.	www.disclosure.com
Discovery Online	www.discovery.com
DKS Interactive	www.dks.com
DoubleClick	www.doubleclick.com
Duracell	www.duracell.com
EDGAR	www.sec.gov/edgar
Emery	www.emeryworld.com
Encyclopedia Britannica	www.eb.com
Epicurious	www.epicurious.com
ESPNET SportsZone	www.espnet.sportszone.com
Excite	www.excite.com
FBI	www.fbi.gov
FedEx	www.fedex.com
Fidelity Instruments	www.fid-inv.com
Firefly	www.ffly.com

About the Author

Chuck Martin was the founding publisher and Chief Operating Officer of *Interactive Age*, the magazine that helped define the interactive marketplace. It was also the first publication to be launched electronically on the Internet simultaneously with the print edition. His experience makes him uniquely qualified to contrast traditional marketing methods (such as direct mail and print advertising) with marketing on the Internet.

Prior to founding *Interactive Age*, Martin was associate publisher of *Information Week* and editor-in-chief of *Personal Computing*. He also served as corporate technology editor of *Time Inc.* and has worked as a journalist at five daily newspapers.

As host of a daily television show on Financial News Network, Martin has interviewed numerous CEOs of leading high-tech companies. He formerly appeared as a co-host of a segment of "Technology Edge," a weekly program on CNBC. He has also appeared as an Internet expert on CNN's "Inside Business."

Martin currently is Vice President, Publishing and Advertising, at IBM in its telecommunications and media industry unit.